My Father's Game

My Father's Game

Life, Death, Baseball

RICK WILBER

McFarland & Company, Inc., Publishers
Jefferson, North Carolina, and London

LIBRARY OF CONGRESS CATALOGUING-IN-PUBLICATION DATA

Wilber, Rick, 1948–
   My father's game : life, death, baseball / Rick Wilber.
     p.   cm.
   Includes bibliographical references and index.

   ISBN-13: 978-0-7864-2984-4
   softcover : 50# alkaline paper ∞

   1. Wilber, Del, 1919–2002.   2. Wilber, Rick, 1948–   .
3. Baseball players—United States—Biography.   4. Fathers
and sons—United States.   5. Terminally ill parents—Care—
United States—Case studies.   I. Title.
GV865.W47W54   2008
796.3570922—dc22   [B]   2007030901

British Library cataloguing data are available

Cover photographs: Del Wilber, Red Sox catcher, with sons
Del Jr. (center) and the author in 1953; later in life the author
and father at the Seahorse Restaurant in Pass-a-Grille, Florida

Manufactured in the United States of America

McFarland & Company, Inc., Publishers
  Box 611, Jefferson, North Carolina 28640
  www.mcfarlandpub.com

For Samantha, Richard Jr., and Robin

Acknowledgments

A WORK OF THIS NATURE RELIES on honesty in both the research and the writing. I have received a great deal of help in both regards.

In my search for an honest understanding of my father's life I relied upon the good graces and memories of a number of family members, including my cousin Donna Wilber, my sisters Mary Smith and Cindy Wilber, and my brothers Del Wilber Jr. and Bob Wilber. I thank them all for their good-faith efforts to tell me the truth as they knew it. I have tried my utmost to be fair in reporting their truths, and any errors in that reporting are my own.

Cousin Donna was traveling with us in Ireland with her two terrific children, Callan and Erik, when my father died; and so she knew through conversation the struggles I'd been having with Dad. Many months later her helpful advice on an early draft of the book was invaluable. Photos from her personal collection were also invaluable, not only for purposes of inclusion in this book but also as historical artifacts that helped me understand the context of my father's youth, including locale, family, education and more.

My older brother Del not only communicated with me often by e-mail, answering questions when he could, but he also sent a short but fascinating memoir that our father had dictated several years before his death. Del had wisely asked Dad to talk about his childhood and his early career in baseball, and so we have a record that would otherwise have been difficult, and perhaps impossible, to reconstruct.

My sister Mary shared a wealth of family photos from the early days of our family's life in baseball, and also talked with me often about what a wonderful grandfather our father had been to her children. I am in her debt for sharing those stories, and am extremely grateful, as well, for her unflinching support during my time spent as Dad's caregiver, when she made regular and lengthy drives to offer her expertise in taking care of difficult parents. She (and my wife, Robin) handled the great bulk of the several monetary issues facing our parents, and did so with unfailing patience, kindness and financial accuracy. The work would have simply been impossible without her. Mary is now the family caregiver for our mother, visiting Mom regularly in a nearby nursing home.

My sister Cindy went to considerable effort to spend time with our father and mother during that difficult year, though her flights from the West Coast to Florida were long and expensive. I am appreciative of the help she gave to me and to our parents and continues to give our aunt (our mother's sister) who is in a nursing home in Texas. I have learned much from Cindy and am thankful for the advice and encouragement she regularly offered, much of it crucial to my efforts to do my best for my parents and so, later, crucial to my writing of this book.

My younger brother Bob shared his memories of those old, better, days when he was a batboy for various minor-league teams that our father was managing. He also told me some interesting stories of his own career in professional and amateur baseball, and I thank him for sharing those stories.

I am indebted to the sharp eyes and useful comments of a number of people who either read the book in manuscript form for purposes of content and factual accuracy, or took the time from their busy lives to be interviewed for details on the caregiving role and my father's last months.

Dr. Joseph Springle, M.D., and Dr. Daniel Bell, M.D., both graciously agreed to lengthy interviews about their respective roles in Dad's health care. Drs. Springle and Bell also read the book in manuscript form and approved those parts where I utilized their expertise. I am grateful for their expert advice. They and the other doctors, nurses, psychologists, physical therapists, receptionists, optometrists, ophthalmologists, social workers and others in Mom and Dad's rather large circle of formal and informal caregivers extended and bettered my parent's lives. My siblings and I owe these people a debt that seems larger than we can repay. I admire them all greatly and thank Springle and Bell, especially, for their advice and support for the book. Any errors in my reportage of their work is, of course, solely mine.

Journalist, author and radio and television personality Pete Williams also read the book in manuscript form and provided me with a sharp-eyed edit, structural advice and thoughtful comments on matters of style and content.

I am especially grateful for the wisdom and good advice I received from my favorite teacher from too long ago, a man I much admire for his writing, editing and teaching skills: William G. Ward. I am but one of his many students to enjoy some success in truth-finding, and we all owe our teacher and mentor our thanks for having known with an intuitively perfect balance how to challenge and yet support us all. Thank you, Bill.

I am also indebted to several professionals in the field who contributed willingly to my understanding of the caregiver role, my father's struggles, my mother's battle with dementia, my own struggles to meet their needs, and my subsequent struggles to understand the sibling anger and disappointment that has come my way as what I can only see as a continuing price to pay for being a caregiver.

Author and eldercare specialist Grace Lebow not only co-authored an outstanding book that helped me through some very difficult times after my father died, she also consented to a lengthy interview and responded to several e-mails. In addition, she read and approved those parts of the manuscript where I utilized her expertise. I learned a great deal from Lebow and am privileged to have her material included in this book. Any errors in my reporting of that work are my own.

In addition to Lebow's book and interview, I learned a great deal about caregiving, eldercare, aging, sibling stress and much more through the close reading of several dozen books, several dozen more websites and more than 100 articles. A wiser man would have read this material before undertaking the caregiver role, or at least in the early innings (as it were). But better late than never, and I owe all these authors and experts a great deal of thanks for having taught me much and guided my hand as I wrote the book. From that lengthy list I pared down the expert advice to a relatively few truly outstanding books and websites, which I list in an appendix.

Baseball player, sports broadcaster, and best-selling author Joe Garagiola has taken on any number of worthy causes in his long and productive life, from fighting against the use by ballplayers of carcinogenic chewing tobacco, to waging financial war against the poverty and hard circumstances of many older players who gave their lives to the game in the days before free agency and baseball's financial boom made millionaires of many players. Garagiola helped start B.A.T. (the Baseball Assistance Team) in the mid–1980s to help those players who were financially unable to meet their housing, health or other basic needs later in life. B.A.T.'s assistance to my father was important to his recovery from one bout with prostate cancer and his subsequent fight against the cancer's return. Garagiola's friendship with Del Wilber began in the 1940s and extended right through to my father's final days. All of us in the Wilber family owe B.A.T. thanks for its support during Dad's final months. Even more importantly, we all owe enormous thanks to Joe Garagiola for his efforts to help his old friend.

A number of other people have been important to my work on this book, including Christopher Scanlan of the Poynter Institute for Media Studies, author and oral historian Peter Golenbock, *Los Angeles Times* columnist and ESPN commentator Bill Plaschke, Dr. Edward Jay Friedlander, director of the School of Mass Communications at the University of South Florida, professor Randy Miller, professor Ken Killebrew (a relative of baseball's famous Harmon Killebrew) and many more.

I owe a large debt to my mother-in-law, Mary Smith, sister-in-law Sue Rea and her husband Bill, and my brother-in-law Thom Smith, all of whom provided the much-needed emotional support and constancy of love and respect that I needed as I struggled through a very difficult and personal challenge in writing this book. They and my immediate family became my most important supporters in what would otherwise have been a very isolated and lonely time. They understood and appreciated what I was trying to do, and I am in their debt for their unwavering encouragement.

Finally, I will always be in debt to my very special son, Richard Jr., and to my brilliant and athletic daughter, Samantha, and to my beautiful and wise wife, Robin, for their patient support during my time as Dad's caregiver and for their continued patience and constant support in the several years after that time that I've spent working on this book. Without them I couldn't have survived the caregiver role. They are the three finest people I have ever known.

Contents

CONTENTS

Preface

IN PART, THIS IS JUST ANOTHER baseball book. In it I talk about my father's career in the game—about the friends he made, the players he coached and managed, the career he carved out for himself, the respect he earned, the love and gratitude of his children for his having raised us inside a sport that means so much to many. He was a good baseball man as a player, coach and scout; he was also a good husband and a loving father. As I point out several times in the book, we had a very special and wonderful childhood as Del Wilber's children, and we knew it and were appreciative. We are all appreciative still.

But dying is hard and my father's final months were a struggle, so this is also a book about the stresses of caregiving.

Nearly by happenstance I was the one of his five children who was nearby as Dad and Mom (or Skip and Taffy, as we've called them for many years) moved into a very good assisted-living facility in St. Petersburg, Florida. Despite the work of the facility's excellent staff, Dad and Mom needed me more than I'd figured on, and I did my best to respond to that need by helping them through the emotional and medical challenges they faced. It turned out to be very hard work.

Almost from the start I wrote a long series of e-mails to my patient brothers and sisters. My original intent was to keep them informed about various issues concerning our parents. But as the months went by, more and more of the e-mails found me venting my frustrations as I grew disappointed and angry with my father and with myself while realizing that Dad was asking more of me than I had to give.

The book is centered on the months when I struggled to be the son that my father and mother needed me to be, but it also gets into the many other aspects of caregiving, including the complications that emerge when an adult takes on the necessary role of part-time caregiver for elderly parents. This means the book is about debts incurred and repaid, about honor and respect, about hard work and love and admiration and disappointment. It's about sibling rivalries, too, and the ripples that splash out from the caregiving role.

I didn't know what a "caregiver" was when I met my parents at the airport and drove them to the assisted-living facility that would be their home for the next year. If someone had asked me to define the term, I would have thought, naturally, that the professional staff at the Fountains at Boca Ciega Bay were the caregivers: the talented and dedicated nurses, aides, administrators, and other staff people who helped my parents — and all of the residents of that large facility — enjoy a quality of life that was the best possible for them under the circumstances. I certainly didn't think of myself as a "caregiver," but that's what I was, as it turned out. Like many millions of other children of elderly parents, I found myself in a role that I wasn't prepared for, and only long after the fact did I come to realize what it meant to be a family caregiver and the definitions and implications of the role.

The book is organized into a series of essays that are very roughly chronological, covering the period when my parents lived together in the assisted-living facility and I was the on-call child for any needs that couldn't be met by the ALF staff (and, often, even for those that *could* be met by the staff). An early chapter also talks about my father's childhood in the Detroit area and his baseball career from high school to retirement. A number of highlights of that career are events that we celebrate still in the extended families that connect to Del Wilber.

Later chapters discuss the caregiver role and include material about that role that I found through extensive research in books, magazine articles and websites. I also did a number of lengthy interviews with care managers and physicians, and portions of those interviews find their way into various chapters. Writing this book also gave me the opportunity to think through my personal understanding of the national pastime and its role as myth for America at large and for the Wilber family in particular.

At the end of the book I offer a readings list of a dozen excellent books and ten major websites for those interested in more information about some of the things discussed in the book. AARP and other sources estimate that more than 20 million adults in the United States serve as unpaid full-time or part-time caregivers for elderly parents. I'm hopeful this book will prove useful and meaningful for a few of those people, and I'm especially hopeful that the book might serve as a decent introduction to the challenges of the caregiver role for those who find themselves taking on the job in the years to come.

The unpalatability of a proposition, however, has no bearing on its truth.

—Richard Dawkins, *Natural History Magazine*,
November 2005

1

Cycling In

It's 1961 and I'm twelve years old and on my way home to get my glove and head up to Tillman school with Dad. I'm late and pedaling hard on my red Huffy bike, the one that's rapidly fading to pink in a blistering St. Louis summer. I've been at the library, a good one, in our suburban town of Kirkwood, Missouri. I've dropped off a couple of juvenile science-fiction novels and browsed the stacks to pick up three more. Russian cosmonauts are circling the Earth, U.S. astronauts are trying to catch up with them, JFK just promised us the moon, and I'm in love with outer-space adventures. Later tonight I'll be under the covers with a flashlight, lost in space with Lucky Starr near the moons of Jupiter. I like science fiction better than anything, including baseball.

But baseball is the family business and obligation and I'm a son of Del Wilber. I've spent my childhood growing up in the dugouts and clubhouses at Fenway and Comiskey and Shibe and elsewhere and just last summer I was the batboy for the Triple-A Charleston Senators. So, even at twelve years of age I know where my priorities are as I pedal hard, trying to worry about flyballs and grounders instead of aliens.

I round the corner from Woodlawn to Woodleaf Court and there's Dad, standing in the driveway, smoking a cigarette, waiting for me. The night before in Kirkwood Park he came to my Khoury League game, which made me a little nervous since he couldn't come often. Late in the game, when it really mattered, a ball came my way in right field and I got under it then

5

started circling while it took forever to come down. Watching it up there in the lights I lost my bearings and then my footing, slipping on the dew-wet grass and falling plop on my rear end as the ball came to earth next to me. The embarrassment was profound.

Today we're going to work on the problem, Dad and I, and I'm excited about that. There are five kids in the family and the youngest is a demanding toddler with asthma problems, so there aren't a lot of chances for me to get personal time with a busy dad, one-on-one. He's not managing some minor-league team this summer; he's scouting instead, and that means he's in town a little more often. Now he wants to spend time playing ball with me, just me, up on the fields at Tillman School: the stars, I'm thinking, are in alignment.

And they stayed that way for that memorable afternoon. I recall with perfect clarity how he walked with me over to the one of the baseball fields, the all-dirt infield rough with rocks and dirt clods, the screen behind home plate bent and rusty and worn. He was a magician with a fungo bat, and I remember him using a fungo to hit me fly balls. Then, when I didn't show much aptitude for that, he brought me into the infield and hit me grounders. I had my hand-me-down glove from Luis Aparicio, the shortstop for the Chicago White Sox who'd befriended me in the clubhouse a couple of years before when Dad was a coach for the Sox. Luis had given me that glove and its magic surely helped me as Dad hit me one-hoppers and shots in the hole. In my memory we played for hours, though I suppose it couldn't have been more than forty-five minutes or so. Using the thin fungo and a couple of dozen baseballs, he put some grounders within reach and others just beyond my outstretched arms, forcing me to work hard to get near them. He hit and I tried to field. Just the two of us. Dozens of groundballs. Some of them went off my chest, some of them slipped under the glove and went into the outfield, some of them I shied away from. Every once in a while we'd pause long enough for me to trot from spot to spot and retrieve the balls I'd missed. Then, after awhile, happily, I started to get a feel for it and we paused less often. I was missing fewer. I began to sense, that day, how and where to move my body, how and where to handle the glove. I began to discover that I wasn't too bad an infielder. I began to discover, in fact, that I was pretty decent. And I liked that, I liked it a lot. Dad talked to me the whole time: keep my feet apart, keep my butt down, keep my glove down and let the ball go into the pocket, move my feet, move my feet, move my feet.

And then we were done and we walked to the car side by side and then he drove us home. Later that summer evening, after I played kick-the-can with the other neighborhood kids until we finally had to call it quits in the darkness, I sat on the couch in the living room, opened up my book and started reading. How was Lucky Starr going to save that anti-gravity engine from sabotage?

It was the summer of 1961 and that was my life: reading and baseball. Life was good. Life was very good.

2

At the End: July 2002

Ex-Philly Del Wilber Dies at 83

The Associated Press 07/19/02 05:09 EDT

ST. LOUIS (AP)—Delbert "Del" Quentin Wilber, who once hit three homers in a game for the Philadelphia Phillies and coached under Ted Williams, has died. He was 83.

The former player, coach and scout died of cancer Thursday at a nursing home in St. Petersburg, Fla., where he moved last summer.

His biggest game was Aug. 27, 1951, the night his daughter Cynthia was brought home from the hospital. Wilber hit three home runs in three at-bats in the Phillies' 3–0 victory over Cincinnati.

Wilber signed with the St. Louis Cardinals in 1941 before serving in the Army Air Force from 1942–45.

He joined the Cardinals' farm club at Columbus, Ohio, in 1946, eventually playing four games in the majors at the end of that season. Wilber played 80 games with the Cardinals over the next three seasons before signing with the Phillies in 1950.

Wilber also caught for the Boston Red Sox before retiring in 1954.

He later coached for three years under Chicago White Sox manager Marty Marion, before serving as a Baltimore Orioles scout. In 1970, he was a coach with the Washington Senators while Williams, his former Red Sox teammate, managed the club.

Wilber was the manager of the Senators' Triple-A Denver team for two years before leading Spokane in the Pacific Coast League in 1973. He later scouted for the Minnesota Twins for more than 15 years.

Survivors include his wife of 59 years, Taffy; three sons, Del Wilber Jr. of McLean, Va., Bob Wilber of St. Paul, Minn., and Rick Wilber of St. Petersburg; two daughters, Cynthia Wilber of Palo Alto, Calif., and Mary Lynn Smith of Orlando, Fla.; a brother and 10 grandchildren.

Funeral arrangements are pending.

On the night my father died I was 4,000 miles from home, leading a group of college students on a study tour through the West of Ireland. For the year before that tour, I'd been Dad's caregiver, spending time with him nearly every day, doing my best for a complicated, unhappy man and his troubled, combative wife. It had been, by a long shot, the most difficult time of my life. Now, for more than two weeks, I'd been away and I'd been enjoying every minute of my break from the challenge of caregiving for elderly parents.

I found out about his death when I walked into Café Internet in Killarney, Ireland, at nine in the morning, got a cup of coffee and then logged on to check my e-mail. There was this from my sister Mary:

Sent: Thursday, July 18, 2002
To: Rick Wilber
Subject: Important...

I just got a call from the Fountains and they are doing CPR on Skip right now ... so it does not look good. I am on my way there now....

Mary...

I knew that had to be it for the old man, and I wasn't surprised. He'd been in bad shape when I'd left, the cancer eating away at his spinal column and his smoker's lungs, the congestive heart just about to go, the Parkinson's wearing him down. He'd been flat on his back, miserable and dying, when I'd last looked in on him, just a few hours before I'd left for Ireland. After the visit I'd gone back to my house, finished packing, and then hurriedly typed this final e-mail to my brothers and sisters.

From: Rick Wilber
Sent: Wednesday, July 03, 2002
To: Update list
Subject: update 07/03/02

I'm leaving in a couple of hours, but I stopped by to see them one more time this morning. Skip complained to me last night on the phone and again today in person about Taffy hitting him. He was very, very weak.

9

I told him I love him. I told him because I don't know that he'll be around when I get back. He looked so weak, and so dispirited, that it's my advice to you to give him a call if you can't come see him. Now's the time, I think, to tell him of our love.

Meanwhile, (the staff) says it's time to move him back down to the nursing-home unit on the first floor. I hinted at him strongly that it was going to happen and he seemed as much relieved as he was unhappy with the news. That unit will cost a little over $100 a day, but I suspect that there is no long run (I surely hope I'm wrong) so let's not worry about the cost. They'll move him down there as soon as possible. I think very, very strongly that he needs to be there, where there's constant care and attention. Maybe, there, he can rally one more time.

I feel guilty as hell, leaving, but there it is.

I'll be in touch by e-mail by tomorrow from Dublin

So I'd known he was about gone and I'd felt guilty about leaving. And I'd left anyway.

On this morning in Killarney there were a dozen more e-mails, but I only opened a few of them. They all said essentially the same thing: the five-hour time difference and Dad's death in the middle of the night in St. Petersburg meant that I needed to catch up. No one said he'd died, but it wasn't hard to figure it out. I got up from the computer, walked over to pay my two-euro bill for the time spent reading the e-mails, then sat down and went through the complicated process of making the international phone call to my sister Mary so I could hear it first-hand. Sure enough, Dad was gone.

We talked for a few minutes and then hung up. My sister had been calm, though when I opened a few more e-mails later that day I found out that Dad had been pretty horrible to her the last night of his life, when she and one of her daughters had paid him a visit: his final words to the two of them had been curses.

But calm and forgiveness are two things my sister Mary is very, very good at. This is a good thing, since she helped out with Dad and Mom for years before I became the family caregiver for the final months. She knew the truth of them in their aging, for better and sometimes for worse, and while I'd always admired her for that from a distance, now that I'd seen the caregiving role up close my admiration for her had become enormous. I didn't know how she'd done it for so long and so well.

I walked out onto New Street. It was 9:15 in the morning and my father had died and it was all I could do for the moment to stand there and watch the tourists walk by.

Dad led a long and often charmed life. He'd been a major-league catcher for the Red Sox, the Cardinals, and the Phillies; a minor-league manager in Denver, Spokane, Louisville, Tacoma, Charleston, and Houston; a scout for the Twins, Orioles, Tigers and A's; a third-base coach for the Washington Senators during their sad final year in the national's capital. He'd been a friend and teammate of the players and coaches of several generations of ballplayers, from the early 1940s to the mid–1980s when he retired. He'd hit home runs off Bob Feller, caught fastballs from Robin Roberts, coached Rod Carew, been a good friend of Stan Musial and Ted Williams and Joe Garagiola and dozens of others. And now he was gone, another player from baseball's golden age to pass away. A week later, Ted Williams would follow him.

I walked back to my bed-and-breakfast to tell my wife and daughter the news. We hugged. I'd asked a lot of them during the year of caregiving: one of the things we'd learned together is how the ripple effect of caring for elderly parents can wash over a family, changing things in ways you'd never expect. As I'd done with my sister, I'd leaned on my family desperately at times and they'd put up with me as my life had filled with disappointment and angry exasperation. They'd handled things with honor and respect and love, these strong women. They'd seen and they knew and they understood.

Which was more than I could say for myself, though God knows I'd tried. Honor, respect, love, understanding: I'd tried for all of those, but often just hadn't been up to it. I didn't have my sister's patience, for one thing; and I couldn't laugh my way through the parental zaniness the way she could, for another. I took it all too seriously in some important ways, and I just flat ran out of that patient forgiveness that my sister and my wife and my daughter seemed to have in abundance.

There was nothing I could do for the moment. I had responsibilities to my fifteen students. They were gone for the day on a bus tour of Dingle, but they'd be back by evening and I'd be in charge. Somehow I had to take care of them and also get back in time for the funeral. It wouldn't be an easy thing to work out. Fretting over that gave me something to do for an hour or two, something to focus on other than the disappointment I felt in myself for not feeling any grief.

By that afternoon my decision had been made for me. My sisters had arranged for a funeral service that wouldn't take place for four or five days and by then I'd be home. The plan was for a small service at the funeral

11

home, a family get-together at a nearby restaurant, and then we would dis-
perse back to our lives. A few days after that my sister Mary and I, the ones
who'd earned the right and wanted the job, would go to Bay Pines National
Cemetery and place Dad's ashes into the ground.

That all sounded fine to me, so after I heard the details I went for a
walk—always a good idea in Ireland in good times or bad—and tried to
sort out my feelings. As many of the millions of Americans who serve as
family caregivers for elderly parents might tell you, this sorting-out was a
complex thing, full of mixed emotions, my sorrow awash in an ocean of
guilt-ridden relief. I'd been blessed with the wonderful childhood that my
father had given his children. We grew up in the clubhouses and dugouts
of baseball's most hallowed halls—Fenway and Shibe and Comiskey and
Sportsman's and a dozen others. As a child I'd stood under Dad's protec-
tive gaze in Fenway during batting practice, glove in hand and my back to
the Green Monster as I eyed a lazy fly ball off the bat of Ted Williams or
Dom DiMaggio. I don't recall ever catching a ball at that age, but later, at
Comiskey where Dad coached for the White Sox, I remember playing pepper with Nellie Fox and Luis Aparicio and then, using the glove that Aparicio gave me when he finished breaking in a new one, I was allowed to be
out there on my own during batting practice, catching balls in the bright
blue sky of a Chicago June day.

It was about as perfect a childhood as a boy could imagine, and I'd
realized it even as I'd been going through it. I can remember sitting in the
green grass of Sarasota's Payne Park on a bright March day in the late 1950s,
eight or nine years old and blinking in the bright sun of spring training, and
glorying in the day. I thought then that I was about the luckiest kid alive,
and maybe I was.

I owed Dad for that and I was more than willing to return the favor by
taking care of him and Mom in their last years. I embraced the idea when
it first came up. I sought their move to the assisted-living facility near my
Florida home. I made a commitment to myself and to them that I'd be there
for them. I shrugged off the warnings from their family physician and from
my own doctor, a friend who'd been honest with me, warning me of the challenge. No problem, I thought, I can handle it. Didn't I raise my Down syndrome son after his mom left us for a guy with a motorcycle? Wasn't that
sweet boy doing great, working at McDonald's and living in a group home
and beating me in one-on-one basketball every Sunday? I figured that if I
could raise a special child like him I could certainly handle a grumpy father.

But I figured wrong. Dad, as it turned out, had been a lot more than grumpy. He'd been a very hard guy to love in that last year and while that was just one year of his 83, it was the one single year of my life and his when I'd seen him almost daily.

Dad's career in the game had kept him gone much of the time as I'd been growing up. He was always traveling with one team or another or, later, on the road scouting or in Florida for the fall instructional league or for spring training. He'd been a distant, if warm, figure for most of my life, so I'd looked forward to getting to know him better, getting to know him like most sons know most fathers. But daily contact with Dad, and with Mom, wore me down; Dad's behavior, especially, abrading my love and compassion bit by bit over the course of those hard months until, when he was gone, I felt only relief.

I could tell from the e-mails I read that my siblings hurt deeply at the news; my brothers, I think, especially so. But their pain was a luxury they could afford. They hadn't done what I'd had to do or seen what I'd seen or heard what I'd heard from Mom and from Dad. For me, the moment had been coming for far too long and with too many difficult days along the way for there to be any grief. I'd heard far too many commands and there'd been too much anger—mine, Dad's, and for one memorable period even Mom's—as I'd struggled with the complexities of my caregiving role. For a year and a few months I was part dutiful son, part stern parent in a hard-to-handle role reversal, part nurse, part cabdriver, part food fetcher, part bottom-wiper and diaper maid, part everything and, too often, part nothing. I felt invisible to the man I was trying so hard to please.

I thought surely I could handle the duties with Dad and Mom, and do these things with a smile, learning from the duties, growing from them, and generally finding the work a positive, worthwhile experience. As it happened, though, I was wrong about most of that and my smile got pretty forced as the months went by. I learned a lot, certainly, but mostly the learning was about my own shortcomings as a caregiver. Dad and Mom in their mutual decline were a pretty combustible mix, as it turned out, and I'd misjudged my own capacity for giving and for handling difficult emotional challenges. The role I embraced turned out to be a damn sight harder than I imagined it would be, and I finally came to think I really wasn't up to it even as I soldiered on, doing what I knew had to be done but suffering all the while.

Thinking this through, I walked along the Muckross Road in Killarney,

13

cloud shadows sliding along the side of Torc Mountain to my right; the shallow, gentle River Flesk straight ahead. The day was calm and cool and, for a change, it wasn't raining. I thought about my father and his crazy demands for attention and time: "And now!" he'd often said on the telephone or in person. So he was gone, and there'd be no more phone-call insanity, no more angry insistence on my being with Him, serving Him (I'd come to capitalize Him routinely in my e-mails to my siblings or, often, calling him Lord Wilber) at the expense of my own family, at the expense of my teaching, my writing, my sanity. No more grappling with the exterior patience and the interior pain. No, that was over at last. And, I told myself, I'd done — or tried to do — the Right Thing for Himself and now it would be easier to do so for Mom.

I'd done the best I could, and I comforted myself with that. My Midwest Catholic upbringing, and especially my Jesuit years in high school, had taught me to honor my father and so I had, I'd been honorable with Dad, though the task of caregiving had been, at its darkest hours, just about more than I could bear.

3

Getting into the Game

MY FATHER WAS BORN IN DETROIT, Michigan, on February 24, 1919, the second child of Delbert and Mary Philomena Quandt Wilber. The Wilbers' first son, Delmar, had died at six months of age and our family lore talks of a strangulated hernia in the umbilical area as the cause of Delmar's death. I'm told my grandmother talked about trying to keep little Delmar warm in the cold Detroit winter by placing him near an open oven. For months he slowly faded before dying, and the emotional trauma of that death seemed to haunt Edna Ma (as we called her) for the rest of her life.

Those years were the heart of the Spanish Flu epidemic which came in the spring of 1918, abated over the summer, and then returned in a deadlier form in the fall of 1918. Somewhere in excess of 600,000 Americans died from the flu that year, including nearly four thousand in Detroit. The death of so many people, many of them children, added to Edna Ma's worry. She became pregnant again shortly after the death of that first son, and the birth of her second baby early the following year smack in the middle of the raging and deadly influenza carnage was surely bittersweet, the joy of a new baby boy tempered by the still-fresh memories of the child they'd lost just months before and the terrible worry that the awful flu might claim this new child. A cousin who was close to Dad's mother for more than twenty years tells me that Dad's mother claimed for the rest of her life to not be aware of that second pregnancy until nearly time to deliver. This denial, my cousin suspects, came from that fear of losing another baby, and it speaks volumes about the sadness and fear and grief she must have felt after losing infant Delmar.

The flu epidemic had been particularly gruesome, as this excerpt from a *Detroit News* historical piece on those years makes clear:

> Panic-stricken citizens demanded laws against public sneezing, coughing or nose blowing. Gauze face masks were issued to soldiers and police, and many ordinary citizens adopted the precaution as well. Possibly, the most sensible precaution was frequent hand-washing.
>
> Newspapers published long lists of the dead. Many who survived contracted tuberculosis, heart diseases, and Bright's disease in their weakened states. Quarantine signs became common. Death wreaths and black bunting draped many homes. Black bunting over the doors and porches told that an older resident had passed away. Grey and white meant that younger family members had died. Passersby understood, but feared to approach to offer condolences. No one blamed them. Funerals became hurried affairs with few attendees.
>
> Coffins piled high near funeral homes often were stolen and used without formality. Bodies placed on porches for daily pickup recalled gruesome scenes from the Medieval Black Plague.*

As my father recalled in his notes about those days, little Delmar was buried in an adult-sized coffin in Detroit's Woodmere Cemetery. Dad guessed the reason for the large coffin was that the cemetery didn't allow baby coffins in certain sections. It is more likely that there was a shortage of coffins even in the early stages of the epidemic and Delmar was buried in whatever coffin could be found.

But, more happily, the new baby, a boy, generally thrived (as would another baby born a few years later on the same date). They named the new son Delbert Quentin Wilber, the middle name coming from the popular youngest son of Teddy Roosevelt, Quentin, a combat pilot who was shot down and killed in July of 1918 flying over the battlefields of World War I. All four of Roosevelt's sons fought with distinction in the war.

A few years later young Delbert did, indeed, catch the flu, and though it was a much milder version his mother wasn't taking any chances and he didn't attend first grade. Dad's mom cherished her eldest boy. Throughout his lifetime she called him "Baby," and then later, "Babe," a nickname that stuck with him through much of his baseball career. Most of his peers thought the nickname came from Babe Ruth. That was, I suspect, a misperception Dad was happy to have.

*Vivian M. Baulch, "When the Flu Ravaged the World," Detroit News *online, http://info. detnews.com/history/story/index.cfm?id=116&category=events*

Young Del Wilber (center) with cousins. (Courtesy Donna Kay Wilber.)

When Dad did go to elementary school he attended the public William Raupp School in Lincoln Park, named after one of the founders of the city. Later, St. Henry's, a Catholic school, opened and Dad went there for one year. As he recalled, that school had no sports and since Dad wasn't much interested in anything other than sports in school, he convinced his parents to put him back in the public school.

During Prohibition in the 1920s Detroit was a hotbed for smuggling. Canada, where liquor was legal, is across the Detroit River from Ecorse, Michigan, just south of Detroit, and Dad grew up in Lincoln Park, the next town in from Ecorse. As Dad told the story, his Grandpa Quandt (his mother's father) had a farm with an obligingly large barn. Quandt had run a local crossroads saloon before Prohibition and willingly made his barn available to the bootleggers once smuggling became a lucrative business. As Dad explained it, "The first storage place for the illegal whiskey was Grandpa Quandt's farm. (The bootleggers) would bring it that far (from the river), stack it in the barn, cover it with straw, and then a couple of days later there would be a big Buick with no back seat in it and they would load up the whiskey and head for Toledo or Chicago."

One of Dad's favorite memories of those days was how he and the other neighborhood kids would head to Quandt's barn to use the discarded back seats from those bootlegger's cars as makeshift trampolines. As Dad said: "We would stand one up straight and lay one flat on the ground and flip and go over it. We had all kinds of fun with those as kids."

Dad was part of an important family. The Quandts had about $40,000 in the bank: revenue, Dad said, from the farm and the storage of the illegal whiskey. As Dad recalled, Grandma Quandt got the money out of the bank before it closed following the stock-market crash of 1929. Dad said that after the repeal of Prohibition the Quandts and their sons and sons-in-law subdivided the eighty-acre farm into lots that became the village and then the city of Lincoln Park. This doesn't square with the city's official history, which says Lincoln Park became a village in 1921 and a city in 1926, so I suspect that the subdivision of the land and the town's growth is what led to the $40,000 in the bank. Dad's memories of his grandmother include her loaning the money out to help the town and its people get through the hard times of the Depression.

As he recalled, "When I started driving, I used to go around and she would be sitting there in the living room on the sofa at the old house, and she would give me a list. She would tell me to take the Buick and go over here on White Street or over there to another street and see if you can get a couple of dollars from these people. She told me that if they haven't got it, don't press them about it or anything. Sometimes I would get a half dollar, sometimes a dollar. I would take it all back and dump it on the table and she would sit there and count it all out. She kept all the tabs but never bothered anybody. Great woman.

"The house is still there, and the Quandt Museum is in City Hall. The house was the original home built in Lincoln Park."

This happy childhood for Delbert and his younger brother, Don, was marred by the hard drinking of the boys' father, my grandfather. I'm told that Grandpa, as we called him, went into angry, drunken tirades that led their mother to take them away at two or three in the morning and put them, for safety, into the nearby home of her sister.

Grandpa's nickname was "Daddy," perhaps reflective of the joy he expressed at the survival of his second and third sons. He was, as a young man, an affable guy and a great storyteller until his mood darkened as he drank. My memories of him include only that amiable nature, his love of fishing, and the cloud of cigarette smoke that swirled around him always. Cigarettes eventually killed him.

While I was never aware of his occasional alcoholic rages, I'm told they lasted most of his life until the evening when he sat next to his granddaughter Donna on the front stoop of the family cottage on Wampler's Lake outside of Detroit. There had been a major confrontation between Grandpa and his wife and their son, Don.

Donna, then fifteen years old, told him that she loved him and that she couldn't stand his drinking anymore. He scared her, she told him.

"Grandpa will quit, Honey," he said to her. "Grandpa will quit."

And he did, so that the last years of his life were sober. Don, his younger son, drank little in adulthood. Del, his older boy and my father, struggled with alcohol like his father had, until the day late in life when he, too, was confronted by a strong, determined woman who laid down the law for him. Like his father, Dad declared himself done with it. Like his father, he was sober for the final years of his life.

Grandpa Del Wilber at age 27, playing for Wyandotte, Michigan. (Courtesy Donna Kay Wilber.)

I have a photograph that shows Grandpa as a young man in a baseball uniform, ready to play. But reading through my father's memories of his youth, the first reference of any kind that I find to baseball is this, about his grandmother on his father's side: "I was a freshman in high school. Grandma Wilber was a great baseball fan. Every day at 3 P.M. a fifteen-minute radio serial would come on called *Betty and Bob.** She had to listen to *Betty and*

One of the earliest of the radio soap operas, Betty and Bob was produced by the famous radio soap-opera team of Frank and Anne Hummert and starred Don Ameche.

Lincoln Park High School, circa 1937, Del Wilber second from right in back row.

Bob, and then she would turn it over to the baseball game, which would then be in about the second inning. She would sit there and listen to that old game all day long."

During his years at William Raupp, Dad had played baseball, basketball and soccer. This was something I wish very much that I'd known in the final year of his life when he attended my daughter's soccer practices and games. I couldn't figure out why he seemed so interested in her youth soccer efforts and only now can I see that his enjoyment was a kind of full circling that I should have understood and appreciated.

In his years at Lincoln Park High School, Dad played football, basketball and baseball. In the first two sports, those were interesting years, he told me, since there were dramatic changes in the style and the rules of the game and Dad was part of those changes. In football, it was during Dad's time at Lincoln Park that the forward pass became increasingly popular and the shape of the ball changed to accommodate that popularity. Dad, a running back and a defensive tackle in those days when players routinely played both offense and defense, became a passer and punter for the Lincoln Park High football team. During his high-school years, Dad said, he became the first student to earn more than ten varsity letters, with three in football, four in basketball and four more in baseball. For the baseball team, he recalled, he was a solid catcher even as a freshman, but it was in his junior and senior years that he became a good hitter, hitting home runs onto the tennis court that edged along the edge of the baseball field in deep left-center. Soon he was playing for the local city semi-pro team and for any other town team he could find. He loved the game and was good at it.

In 1937, he became the second member of the large, extended Wilber family to graduate from high school. Shortly thereafter, with no desire for college, Dad took a job in the stockroom of Ford Motor's River Rouge assembly plant. At Ford he also played for the company basketball team and in those pre–NBA days industrial-league basketball was about as high a level as there was. His father got him the stockroom job and Dad was grateful in those Depression days, but it was hard, physical work and Dad admitted to me that he didn't much care for it. When he saw a small filler in one of the sports columns of the Detroit Free Press that said that the St. Louis Browns were holding a try-out camp in Springfield, Illinois, he decided he had to give that a shot. He convinced a friend, George Hill, to drive with him to Springfield for the weekend. Hill was also a good ballplayer, a pitcher, and, most importantly, owned an automobile.

They parked the Model A Ford outside the ballpark in the middle of the night and slept in it until the camp started the next morning. Wearing their town-team uniforms, they were battery mates for the first innings of the tryout game that took place later that morning. Immediately after their stint, the boys were approached by two Browns scouts who said they wanted the boys back the next day. When Dad and Hill admitted that they had no place to stay or money to spend on a hotel, the scouts put them up in a boarding house and bought them dinner. The next day Hill pitched another inning and Dad caught four. After a nervous few hours watching dozens of other hopefuls play, the two were asked to come to the Leland Hotel in Springfield where they got just about the best news an athletic teenager could get in 1937: they were being offered contracts from the St. Louis Browns to be professional ballplayers. Both boys had to take the contracts home and get them signed by their parents.

Searching through the family archives for material for this book I came across the original correspondence for that contract and others. Though he never told me about this, Dad apparently approached several teams following his high-school graduation to ask for a try-out. Manager Hap Bohl (a successful minor-league player and manager during the 1930s) wrote this on Fremont (Ohio) Reds stationery on June 12 of 1937:

> Dear Delbert:
>
> I have your letter of recent date and am pleased to hear of your fine showing.
>
> You can, of course, come down for a trial any time you wish, but my sincere advice to you would be to go to college. It isn't everyone that gets such an opportunity and if you do not accept the offer to go to college you may greatly regret such a decision later in life. College is like anything else, you get out of it just what you put in. So if you go devote yourself to it and I'm sure it will not be a waste of time.
>
> Keep in touch with me and let me know how you are doing in Baseball.
>
> Very sincerely yours,
> Hap Bohl

When I first read this letter I was surprised to see the mention of college. Dad had always indicated to me that he'd never considered college but had planned on working at the Ford plant and giving baseball a try. This letter, though, implies that some college wanted him as an athlete or as a student.

A letter from nearly a month later, on San Antonio Missions letterhead, shows the response to a letter Dad sent inquiring about that tryout in Springfield. The Missions played then, as now, in the Texas League and were a minor-league team in the St. Louis Browns' organization.

> July 15, 1937
>
> Dear Wilber:
>
> This will acknowledge receipt of your letter of recent date, which has reference to our Baseball Training Camp to be held in Springfield, Illinois, beginning July 26th.
>
> The requirements are that every player must be between the ages of 17 and 21; at least, five feet nine inches tall, and weigh 150 pounds or more. You must furnish your own shoes, glove and uniform, and will also have to furnish your own transportation to camp and pay your living expenses while there. The camp will last three or four days.

22

Del Wilber, catcher, Findlay, Ohio, circa 1938.

Trusting that you will be abe (able) to avail yourself of this opportunity to attend our Training Camp, I am

> Yours very truly,
> Gary Airep
> Vice-President

P.S. Should you attend our camp and show sufficient ability to warrant your being tendered a contract for the 1938 Season, transportation to your home from Springfield will be refunded you, and also your board and room while attending camp.

He did attend that camp, of course, and was successful. The Browns organization scouts were there and liked Dad's skill and offered him that contract, which he was to take home and have his parents sign. The contract called for $60 per month during the 1938 season. It wasn't much, but it was professional baseball. I have two more letters from that time period. In the first, dated August 3, 1937, Browns' Assistant Vice-President G.E. Gilliland tells Dad that the Browns have received the contract signed by Dad's parents, but Dad had forgotten to sign it himself. Gilliland asks him to sign it and send it back to the Browns in the envelope provided. He then says, "We are mighty happy to have you as a member of the Browns' organization and you may rest assured you will be given every opportunity to make good with one of our clubs next spring. You will be notified around the middle of March or the first of April when and where we want you to report."

Another letter from Gilliland, dated fifteen days later, reports that the signed contract has been received and says again that he's confident that Delbert Wilber will have every opportunity to prove himself as a ballplayer. Dad retired from baseball in 1986, nearly fifty years later, so Gilliland's confidence was well-placed.

In 1938 Dad played for the Findlay, Ohio, Browns in the Ohio State League. The playing surface, he once told me, was so full of holes and bumps that it was dangerous to play on. In 1939 he again played for Findlay, and then in 1940 he was traded to the St. Louis Cardinals organization and moved up a class to play in Springfield, Missouri. Then the following year, 1941, he played in Columbus, Georgia.

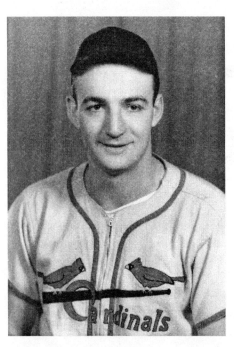

Del Q. Wilber, a young Cardinal, circa 1941.

Dad was lucky to find himself in the Cardinal organization. In the 1930s and into the 1940s, Branch Rickey, who'd grown up on a farm in Missouri, conjured up baseball's minor-league "farm" system as a way to produce talent for his Cardinals. Dad benefited from Rickey's determination to grow talent in a large system of minor-league teams (in 1940 the Cardinals owned thirty-two minor-league teams and had working agreements with eight more*) that fed the best of their players to the major-league team. Later, Dad would discover another aspect of Rickey's system when he was sold to the Phillies for cash. Rickey's farm

---

*Jules Tygiel, Past Time: Baseball as History (New York: Oxford University Press, 2001), p. 93.

system worked because the players who were good enough to be big-leaguers but not good enough to win a spot in the Cardinals line-up were sold to other teams for cash, which helped fund the entire Cardinals franchise.

In 1941 Dad figured that four years of seasoning in the minors had him ready for a shot at the big leagues and the Cardinals seemed inclined to agree, offering him a big-league contract for the following spring training. But Pearl Harbor changed everything for him, as it did for most of America's professional baseball players. In 1942 he was drafted into the then–Army Air Corps. He reported to Jefferson Barracks, Missouri, and began basic training as a glider pilot. He played baseball, too, at Jefferson Barracks, he told me not long before he died. He said that he'd been the catcher for a base team that had several exhibition games against the famous Homestead Grays of the Negro Leagues. The game was played on a field in nearby Belleville, Illinois. Satchel Paige and Josh Gibson were on that team, Dad recalled.

But outside of the moments of baseball relief, Dad didn't care for glider-pilot training, which wasn't as glamorous as he might have hoped. As he recalled in his notes, "We would practice in wooden gliders and sit there in full uniform and then all of a sudden the doors would fly open and they would say 'Everybody out!' and we would play war games." Then, he said, they would do the same routine again. And again.

In those days the would-be glider pilots trained as enlisted men and spent the initial portion of their basic training learning to be glider infantry, a role they would be in once they'd landed in battle, since gliders provided a one-way trip. Dad was six-foot-two and 200 pounds at the time, and in good shape from playing professional ball. He might not have liked the glider corps all that much, but he was apparently good at the job, working his way from private to corporal and then to drill sergeant, where he was in charge of 142 men training to glide into battle in flimsy, wooden, engine-less aircraft.

The glider-borne infantry participated in some of World War II's most harrowing battles, including the initial pre-dawn landings behind German lines in Normandy and the ambitious but flawed Operation Market-Garden. In both cases casualties among the glider troops were very high.

But Dad never took part in those actions. Instead, the war changed for him when baseball intervened, as it did so often in his life. Over his life-time, Dad's attachment to baseball altered his life for the better any number of times and, once or twice, for the worse. None of those life-altering moments was more important than the day at Jefferson Barracks when a major approached him and asked if he was Del Wilber, the ballplayer who'd been a catcher in Columbus the year before. The major, a chaplain, was a baseball fan. He wanted to know how Dad had scored on the IQ entrance test administered to all draftees. Dad had scored a 123. The major asked him to take it again, and if he could score a 125 or better he'd see about getting Dad into officer-candidate school with the goal of becoming a physical training instructor for some of the thousands of pilot candidates who would soon be learning to fly and fight for the Army Air Corps. Dad scored a 126 on that retake and then went before a board of officers who assessed his ability. They knew he was a professional athlete and so perhaps that influenced the questions, the first of which was "What is Emkee's rug"? Dad responded that Emkee's rug was the tarpaulin developed by Howard Emkee, a Philadelphia Athletics pitcher who'd gone into the tarpaulin business.

The next question was "Who is John Kimbrough?" Dad knew that Kimbrough was a bruising running back at Texas A&M known as "Jarrin' John," who'd been the star of the 1941 Cotton Bowl. More questions followed but the pattern had been established and Dad was on his way to becoming a 90-day wonder at Officer Candidate School at Miami Beach.

There were thousands of such candidates, of course, and they came from all walks of life. In his dictated notes, Dad recalled that Officer Candidate Clark Gable was just across the hall. Gable was in Miami Beach at OCS at that time, so it is very possible that he was, in fact, a few doors down from Dad.

Dad made it through OCS and was assigned to Randolph Field in San Antonio, Texas. Just two days after arriving at Randolph he was assigned to the San Antonio Aviation Cadet Center's Squadron 104 in the pre-flight school at Kelly Field. He spent his war mostly right there, getting cadets into shape for the fight they would soon be facing.

As Dad recalled, about one lonely month after arriving in San Antonio, he saw a picture in the local paper of a girl who worked on the air base and had just been named Miss Air Force San Antonio.* He asked a friend

---

*We have a newspaper clip, unfortunately trimmed so that the date and the name of the paper aren't included, that says: "In response to the lovely New York girl recently selected as 'Miss Air Force of New York,' Duncan Field has selected Miss Edna Mae Bennett, 18, employee in the personnel department, as 'Miss Air Force San Antonio.'" Duncan Field was adjacent to, and part of, Kelly Field, which had been an Air Corps aviation training center since 1917.

who was dating a girl from Kelly Field to find out if his girlfriend knew this beauty and she did. Dad got the girl's phone number and then put considerable effort into convincing her that he was worth a date. That spring they went to the Majestic Theater in San Antonio to see Gary Cooper in *Pride of the Yankees*, which provided the perfect opportunity for Dad to let her know that he was a promising ballplayer. Happily for Dad, Eddie (as she was then called) had parents who were baseball fans and gave their blessing to the relationship. On December 21, 1943, they were married in San Antonio and spent their honeymoon at a dude ranch in Bandera, Texas. Dad had a three-day pass to get married, and his brother Don, who was in training at Randolph, was the best man.

Don Wilber went to the Pacific as one of the famous Ken's Men of the 43rd Bomb Group of the Fifth Air Force. Don entered the service after graduating from Lincoln Park High School in 1943. After training in San Antonio he was assigned to the Philippines. He was not so athletic as his older brother and his interests since he was young had been in reading and in photography: by the time he was eleven years old he had a darkroom in the family basement. When he arrived at Clark Air Base in the Philippines he mentioned his interest in photography and was immediately assigned to take before and after shots of bombing targets and to work in the developing labs. I'm told he found it fulfilling, though it could be harrowing work when he was assigned to fly over targets before and after the bombs were dropped. His children tell me he never spoke much about the dark side of those times, but, instead, focused his memories on the Filipino people that he met and liked. Later, he was assigned to the island of Ie Shima. He was on that island when the most famous war correspondent of them all, Ernie Pyle, was killed when his jeep hit a mine not far from where Don was working in a darkroom lab.

At war's end, Don was mustered out and returned home on January 6, 1946. That same week one of his girlfriends from high school introduced him to the pretty Patricia Boyle at a party at Marygrove College in Detroit. A few months later he and Pat were married and four children, three daughters and a son, followed over the next ten years. Don died from complications of lung and bladder cancer on January 9, 1994, forty-eight years to the day from the time he met his wife after coming home from serving his country.

While his brother Don was busy in the Pacific Theater of the war, my father was playing baseball. As player/manager of the Cadet Training Center

Warhawks, Dad's job was to play baseball and so boost morale among the troops. Dad must have impressed his superior officers to get the job as manager. There were a lot of other players with more experience, but it was Del Wilber, a minor-leaguer still trying to make the big leagues, who got the job. On his team were Enos Slaughter and Howard Pollet, Cardinal teammates before the war. Slaughter was a star, of course, and Pollet won three games in the 1944 Service League playoffs and was named the most valuable player.

It wasn't a bad way to spend the war, but perhaps it was disappointing, as well. Players like Yogi Berra, Hoyt Wilhelm, Bob Feller, Warren Spahn and others were in the thick of the action. Berra was on a rocket-launcher off Utah Beach on D-Day, Wilhelm earned a Purple Heart in the Battle of the Bulge, Feller was an anti–aircraft gunner on the battleship *Alabama*, and Spahn was a combat engineer during the Battle of the Bulge.

But the great majority of major-leaguers played baseball while they were in the service, serving their country by playing the game and, in the case of Dad and some others, teaching physical education. As Slaughter noted in a story in the *San Antonio Express* in July, 1995, "I had 600 cadets in every

Top and bottom: **Edna Mae Bennett, soon to be Mrs. Del Wilber, circa 1943. (Courtesy Mary Smith.)**

28

Don Wilber (right) in the Pacific, circa 1944. (Courtesy Donna Kay Wilber.)

class, and we'd run and do calisthenics, work the cross bar, do wind sprints....
I tried to do a good job."

For the Cadet Center team, Slaughter hit .498 in 1943 and .420 in 1944
as the Warhawks won the service-league championship both those years and
the next one, as well. Then Slaughter and others left the Cadet Center to
tour re-captured islands in the Pacific, entertaining troops who'd fought
hard and suffered and deserved some entertainment. Playing on makeshift
fields cut from coral and sand, Slaughter and his teammates played ball in
front of crowds of thousands of worn-out soldiers. It must have been a joy
for many of those men to see their major-league heroes from pre-war days
right there in front of them, playing baseball on a tiny dot of an atoll in the
South Pacific.

My father was Pollet's catcher and the team's player/manager, and it
must have been something to be a twenty-four-year old 1st lieutenant who
was also the manager of a baseball team that featured major-league stars.

29

Enos Slaughter, unidentified soldier, and manager Del Wilber look over the lineup for the San Antonio Aviation Cadet Center Warhawks.

Dad's success did not go unnoticed. I have a letter from St. Louis Cardinal President Sam Breadon from February of 1946 where he offers my dad a contract.

Dear Del:

Enclosed find your contract for the 1946 season, calling for FOUR THOUSAND ($4000.00) DOLLARS, as agreed to on the 'phone today. Also check for $66.20 covering transportation from your home to St. Petersburg, Florida. Please sign and return one copy of contract to us.

I want to thank you for all the nice things you did for the Cardinals boys in the Service while you were in San Antonio.

Will be glad to see you when I get to St. Petersburg.

Sincerely yours,
Sam Breadon
President

30

S.A.A.C.C. manager Del Wilber, unidentified soldier, and Enos Slaughter, San Antonio, 1943.

Four thousand dollars wasn't a lot of money by major-league standards, even then (my wife, a college finance professor, puts it at about $40,000 in today's dollars); but it wasn't bad for a guy who'd never played a game in the big leagues and had lost five years of his youth to the military. More importantly for Dad, I'm sure, it was an opportunity to get started on the promising career that had been on hold for the war years.

He didn't stick with the big club, though. The Cardinals had a surplus of catchers in the late 1940s, including a talented (and younger) Joe Garagiola and Del Rice. In 1946 Dad had just four at-bats, didn't get a single hit, and spent all but a few days of the season in Columbus, Georgia. There he did fine, but it must have been disappointing to keep an eye on the Cardinals from afar in that famously successful year for the team. The Cardinals became world champions in 1946 when Slaughter, back from touring the Pacific Theater, made his famous "mad dash" around the bases. Red Sox outfielder Johnny Pesky was criticized by the sportswriters for having inexplicably held the ball on that play, though the truth is more complicated than that, as it is for any number of baseball's myths.

In 1947 Dad did a little better for the Cardinals, appearing in fifty-one games,* and getting twenty-three hits in ninety-nine at-bats. Eight of those hits were doubles, so he was becoming more productive at the plate. That year he shared catching duties with Joe Garagiola and Del Rice, though manager Eddie Dyer wasn't that happy with any of them ("One can't hit, one can't catch and one can't throw," was his famous assessment of the three). In a story I have from the *New York Times* from August of 1947, Dyer complains about the catching spot, though at that point the Cardinals were in the pennant race and facing an important series against the Brooklyn Dodgers. The Cards faded, so Dad missed his chance for a World Series ring, but his good play earned him another year. In 1948 though, he appeared in just 27 games and hit a dismal .190.

In 1949 Dad was sent to the Texas League as player/manager for the Houston Buffaloes. Then, in 1950, he was assigned to the Rochester Red Wings of the International League. It must have looked like his playing career was winding down, but in Rochester he revived his fortunes and his career by doing a solid job as the starting catcher and hitting well, helping the Red Wings win the International League pennant. In one memorable

*Cardinal pitcher Murray Dickson preferred Del Wilber catching behind the plate, and Dad often credited Dickson for helping him reach the big leagues and stick there in 1947.

mid–August Red Wings game against Jersey City he caught all twenty-two innings of a marathon win. Incredibly, in that game both pitchers, Tom Poholsky for Rochester and Andy Tomasic for Jersey City, went the distance, each pitching for more than five hours before the game finally ended.

Dad capped off that fine season with winter ball in Havana, catching for the Havana Leones (also called the Reds) and playing alongside a few other Americans including Hoyt Wilhelm. I have a few faint memories of that Havana winter, though my recollections are tainted, no doubt, by photographs and home movies from those days.

In Havana he started well

Del Wilber, Cardinals, circa 1947.

but eventually struggled and lost his starting spot. For that winter season he played in 54 games and had 37 hits in 150 at-bats for a .247 average with three home runs. Those aren't great numbers, but the caliber of baseball was outstanding and so his winter in Havana paid off when the Cardinals traded Dad to the Philadelphia Phillies, who'd taken note of his play for the Reds and for Rochester the summer before and were thinking he might be their starting catcher.

He didn't get that starter's job for the Phils, but he had a pretty good season, his best in the majors, playing in eighty-four games, getting to the plate two hundred and forty-five times, with sixty-eight hits for a .278 batting average with eight home runs: three of them on August 27, when his newborn daughter Cynthia came home from the hospital while Dad, in the second game of a double-header, took Ken Raffensberger downtown (or dialed eight, or went yard, or whatever baseball jargon suits you best) three different times.

That three home-run day is something we've made much of in our

33

DELBERT (DEL) WILBERT: Catcher.
Batea y tira a la derecha. Estatura 6' 2".
Pesa 200 libras. Nació en Lincoln Park,
Mich., el 24 de Febrero de 1919. Casado.
Tiene 2 hijos. Comenzó a jugar base ball
en 1938-39 con el Findlar, de la Ohio
State League. En 1940 jugó con el club
Springfield, y en 1941 con el Columbus,
de la American Association. De 1942
al 45 fué al servicio de la Armada de los
Estados Unidos. En 1946 ingresó nueva-
mente en el Columbus y a fines del mis-
mo año pasó al St. Louis Cardenals, de
la Liga Nacional, donde estuvo hasta
1948. En 1949 fué a jugar al club Houston, de_la Texas League. Y en 1950 jugó
con el club Rochester, de la International
League, donde terminó con un average
de 299. Es la primera vez que viene a jugar base ball a Cuba, con el club Habana.

DELBERT WILBERT

Del Wilber, Havana Reds, 1950-51. (Courtesy Cesar Lopez.)

family. Growing up, every day for many years I walked by the framed cer-
tificate that read "Big-League Baseball's Only Perfect Day" and then gave
the line score and the details of that afternoon's success. I thought it was
something pretty special, an achievement of note. Which it is; but not by
much, really, in terms of big-league standards. Nearly six hundred big-
leaguers have hit three homers in a game, many of them hitting them con-
secutively and many others having hit three in one game multiple times.
Dave Kingman did it five times; Johnny Mize six times.

Why then has this achievement loomed so large for us as a family?
Well, for starters, it's not something that most children can claim for their
fathers. In our neighborhood in suburban St. Louis, the fathers were all
good men living good lives and raising good children. But those fathers were
never big-leaguers, never sat in the clubhouse in Fenway and chatted with
Ted Williams about getting together for a drink, or talked with Robin
Roberts or Howie Pollet or Murray Dickson or any of the dozens of other
pitchers that Dad caught about what pitches were working well. So that
which was ordinary by big-league standards was extraordinary, indeed, by
neighborhood standards.

34

More importantly, I think, hitting those three home runs in Philadelphia on an August afternoon put Dad into a category which, while large, was also exceptional. Sure, Del Wilber was a journeyman, a mediocre player by big-league standards. In fact, he had just eight home runs for that season, and that puts him into another interesting list: players with three-homer games who had fewer than ten home runs for the season, including the likes of Mickey Cochrane, Babe Ruth (in 1935), Pete Rose, Jason Varitek, Gene Oliver and others: a total of some thirty-three players. But the lengthy list of ballplayers who hit three home runs in one game includes names like Orlando Cepeda, Dale Murphy, Boog Powell, Cal Ripken Jr., Ruth, Ted Williams, Carl Yastrzemski, Duke Snider, Gil Hodges, Rogers Hornsby, Ernie Banks, Sammy Sosa, Ted Kluszewski, Johnny Bench, Pete Rose, Rocky Colavito, Ty Cobb, Hank Aaron, Harmon Killebrew, Lou Gehrig, Joe DiMaggio, Roberto Clemente, Stan Musial, Mark McGwire, Willie Mays and Barry Bonds. That's pretty good company to keep, and Dad was happy and proud, I know, to have earned his way into that club. In terms of the Philadelphia Phillies, the list is sixteen names long and right there alphabetically on the list between Mike Schmidt in 1987 (one of three times he did it) and Cy Williams in 1923 is Del Wilber, August 27, 1951.

Nice job, Dad.

After that solid year for the Phils, Dad must have felt like he'd earned a spot on the roster for 1952 and, indeed, he started that season with the Phillies. But after appearing in just two games he was traded to the Red Sox, where he spent the next three seasons as a back-up catcher and, more importantly, a pinch-hitter. In 1952 he

Topps 1952 Reprint Series, card # 383: Del Wilber.

35

appeared in forty-seven games for the Sox, had 135 at-bats and hit a respectable .267. The following year he appeared in fifty-eight games, had 112 at-bats, had twenty-seven hits and, remarkably, had twenty-nine runs batted in. In the history of major-league baseball fewer than a dozen players have totaled more runs batted in than hits in a season (with 100 or more at-bats), so that, like his three home-run day, puts Dad in pretty interesting company. One highlight for that year came early when on May 6 and May 10 he hit consecutive pinch-hit homeruns for the Sox.

But he was thirty-four and getting old for the game by then and though he made the Red Sox roster in 1954 it wasn't much of year; he appeared in just twenty-four games with sixty-one at bats and only eight hits and on that unhappy note his playing days came to an end when he was traded to the Giants and wound up instead as a coach for the White Sox in 1955 and 1956, working for his friend and fellow St. Louisan and ex–Cardinal Marty Marion, who managed in Chicago for those two seasons.

After that, Dad scouted for the Baltimore Orioles and then managed in the minors for a while. I have a clip of a column from February of 1958 by famous sportswriter Shirley Povich that talks about Dad's one famous signing as a scout, when he was the one who got bonus baby Dave Nicholson to sign with the Orioles. Povich says in the

Del Wilber and author, Charleston, W.Va., 1960.

column that Orioles "like their deal for Nicholson well enough to give the scout who signed him, Del Wilber, the job as manager of their Louisville farm team as a reward." I hadn't known that the Louisville job was a reward for the Nicholson signing, but I remember well our family's summer in Louisville, where we lived in a motel near the ballpark and where I remember spending most of my time wandering around under the stands with several other children of players or front-office personnel.

After that Dad managed in Charleston, W.Va., where I had my one golden summer as batboy of Dad's Charleston Senators. That Triple-A team

Del Wilber, Florida Instruction League manager in Bradenton, Florida.

for the then Washington Senators was a club filled with players who would, a few years later, be stars for the American League pennant-winning Minnesota Twins. Zoilo Versalles, Jim Kaat and others were on that team and were nice to me. I spent the summer in the clubhouse, listening to my cleats clatter on the chewed wood of the slats that covered the concrete floor of the tunnel that led from the clubhouse to the dugout. To me, that's the sound of baseball, more so than any crack-of-the-bat or roars of the crowd clichés.

The next year Dad was a scout, and he spent most of the 1960s in that role for the Twins, most often scouting other major-league teams for possible trade material for the Twins. Dad managed the Twins' team in the fall Florida Instructional League, too, in those years and he gave me the gift of one other baseball experience when I attended a local junior college in Bradenton, where Dad's team was training and playing. I was allowed to work out with some of the Twins rising stars and the occasional visiting veteran. One memorable day I got the chance to pitch to Rod Carew, who'd come to Bradenton's McKechnie Field to work on a few things prior to changing his defensive positioning for the Twins. I thought of myself as a pretty promising college pitcher at the time and, as I recall, I got Carew, one of the best hitters the game has ever seen, to swing and miss once or twice at my junior-college curveball. If my vivid memory of this is correct, on his third swing he hit a line-drive to deep left center that never seemed to get more than ten feet off the ground as it traveled some 350 feet, bounced once off the warning track, then caromed loudly off the outfield wall. I suspect there is still a dent in the outfield wall at McKechnie from the force of that blow.

In 1970 Dad had a brief return to on-field coaching with the Washington Senators during Ted Williams' time as manager. A clip I have from *The Washington Post* from that year is a column by Merrell Whittlesey that talks about Dad's storytelling and group-cooking abilities, calling him "the quiz master, the chef, and the fellow who could have written the Baseball Encyclopedia from memory if he had been asked." The column notes that Williams and the Senators organization made Dad an on-field coach for eighty-five days so he could qualify for the modern phase of baseball's pension. The extra on-field days moved him from the original phase and so doubled his benefits, making him a nine-year veteran. That doubling of benefits was a matter of some considerable importance nearly fifteen years later when Dad retired, and loomed even larger during the final years of his life and even today for his widow, who benefits from the quality of care she can afford in large part because of Williams and the Senators and their largesse in 1970. This is proof again of several important aspects of Dad's life in baseball. First, he was liked and often admired; through his genial charm he built a lifetime of friendships in the game. Next, Dad, like many ballplayers, benefited from baseball's sense of family. The game tries to take care of its own in ways both small and large and through mechanisms that are formal and informal. Baseball operates on the phone-call system still, I suspect, where the family of a ballplayer enjoys certain unwritten benefits ranging from the trivial, like free admission to most games, to the more significant, like multiple chances for the son or sons of a player to get a chance to play the game themselves.

In our family my older brother—an outstanding college player at Purdue—was so good that he didn't need that help. In 1965 he led the Big Ten in homeruns, runs-batted-in and slugging percentage and by June he'd signed with the Phillies. After a month in Miami in the Florida State League he moved to Spartanburg, South Carolina, and from there to Huron, North

Dakota. Then he played in Portsmouth, Virginia, before moving to Bakersfield, California; all of this the typical wanderings of a minor-leaguer doing well as he struggles to approach the big leagues. Ultimately real life (and a draft deferred job in that Vietnam era) meant quitting baseball and getting on with raising a family and building a career, mostly in sports management and promotions. He's done extremely well in both regards—family and career—and I admire him.

It is interesting that he has the same sorts of stories to share as our father did. There's the time he played in his first professional game for Miami and a guy named Johnny Bench was catching for Tampa. After the game my brother called Dad to tell him about going two for three and driving in the winning run and Dad, then a scout for the Twins, asked about this Bench kid's talent. My brother remembers thinking Bench wouldn't make it to the big leagues because his thighs were too big. Then, in Spartanburg, he played against Bobby Bonds and Al Oliver and was a teammate of Larry Bowa. He even faced the young Nolan Ryan, who was pitching for Greenville. He recalls going 0 for four against Ryan, but remembers with some considerable pride that he did not strike out. In North Dakota he played against Reggie Jackson, and in a rehab session (for a spike wound) he spent time in the training room with Bill White. Memorably, in 1966 while at Spartanburg he batted against Satchel Paige.

My younger brother's career was one of struggle. In college, at Southern Illinois University at Edwardsville, he had just fourteen at-bats his sophomore year and had three hits, for a .214 average. That year, though, the Cougars made it to the finals of the Division II College World Series. His junior year, when the team again advanced deep into the NCAA Division II playoffs, he did better, playing in forty games as a starting outfielder and hitting a more respectable .264. His senior year the team was less talented and finished well under .500. My brother's average for the thirty-one games he played in was .208. While he struggled to hit for average his glove was good in the outfield and his arm excellent, so those skills and some telephone calls by Dad got him a shot in the low minors, where he did all right in Lakeland, Florida; then Paintsville, Kentucky; then Medford, Oregon, before moving on into real life. Dad made the right phone calls to get him those opportunities, but a serious injury and that weak hitting ultimately ended his minor-league career. Four years later, playing for an outstanding amateur team, he blossomed and enjoyed considerable success, but the professional days were done.

The Denver Bears win the pennant in 1971.

But comparing his career to my own makes my younger brother look positively Ruthian in comparison. To find out why you can do a Google search (as I did) for my name and you'll see a lot of writing references and then, somewhere on the second or third page of the references you'll find my lifetime college statistics as a pitcher and hitter: In 1969 at Southern Illinois University–Edwardsville I had three at-bats and two hits. I pitched in eight innings and gave up fifteen earned runs, for an ERA of 16.87.

You can see why writing seemed to me like a better option than baseball. Or basketball, where my college statistics are at about the same level of absurdity as my baseball stats. I scored twenty-one points in my one year of play, ten of them through free throws where I hold the trivial record of having hit on all ten of my opportunities from, as the sportswriters would say, the charity stripe. None of Del Wilber's sons, in short, had his gifts or his good fortune when it came to baseball.

In 1971 Dad returned to the minor-leagues to manage and enjoyed success through much of that decade. His 1971 Denver Bears were in first place from the first day of the season to the last with a record of 73 wins and 67 losses and won the American Association's Western Division and then won the league's championship before losing in the Junior World Series. In 1972 he again managed the Bears, who didn't do as well that year, winning 61 and losing 79. There were some talented players on those Denver teams, including future big-leaguers Mike Thompson, Richie Scheinblum and Jeff Burroughs.

In 1973, Dad managed the Spokane Indians of the Pacific Coast League and led the team to a pennant. The 1973 team featured Bill Madlock who soon became a big-leaguer and a good one, winning four batting championships. More importantly for Dad, 1973 was also the year he caught baseball's brass ring and became a big-league manager. In early September of that year Dad's Spokane Indians had just won their pennant when the big club, the Texas Rangers, fired manager Whitey Herzog and Dad was named interim manager. Newspaper clips I have from that day talk about Herzog's disappointment at being fired, despite the team's 47–91 record.

"I was under the impression that I had a two-year contract and was in a position of trying to build a ball club," Herzog is quoted as saying when he got the news. The same clip, from the *New York Times*, says Rangers owner Bob Short is talking to Billy Martin, the controversial manager of several teams and himself recently fired from his managing duties with the Detroit Tigers. Other clips from other papers seem to indicate that Del Wilber would finish out the season as the Rangers manager and then become one of the prime candidates for the permanent job. I even have a personal note dated September 8, 1973, on Milwaukee Brewers' letterhead, from Cal Ermer, then coaching for the Brewers. "Congratulations! Win 'em all. You deserve the opportunity; make the most of it. Let me know if I can help you in any way. Wishing you much success and happiness. Sincerely, Cal Ermer."

But that's not how it happened. Instead, after that one game (a win, 10–8, over the Oakland A's) Dad's interim duties ended and Short, no surprise, hired Martin to manage the club. Ironically, Cal Ermer, too, was once fired and replaced by the volatile but often successful Martin.

Dad returned to Spokane the next season and led the Indians to their second consecutive pennant. Then in 1975 and 1976 he returned to scouting for the Twins and managing in the Fall Instructional League. In 1977 he gave managing one last shot when he was named manager of the Tacoma Twins of the Pacific Coast League, but the Tacoma managing stint was his last and did not go well. After a decent start the Twins lost eleven out of fourteen games during a June and July slump and the major-league Twins farm director George Brophy—a good friend of Dad's—fired him and named Tom Kelly the player-manager. Kelly had been in the big leagues as a player for the proverbial cup of coffee, but after his start in managing in Tacoma he went on to become a successful major-league manager, guiding to the Twins to a couple of World Series appearances and winning more than one-thousand games.

Some clips I have from the *Tacoma News Tribune* about Dad's firing seem to indicate that Dad was ready to leave. "To tell you the truth, I'm a little relieved," he says in one article. "My wife has been ill," he adds, "and I haven't been able to be with her. I have a new grandbaby I haven't seen. I'm going home after returning to Tacoma to pack my bags, and I'll start looking for a new job."

The players who are quoted in the article take the blame on themselves, of course, for the team's failings. First baseman Randy Bass (who made it to the big leagues for six seasons after his time in Tacoma) says, "We're not going good, everybody knows that. But it didn't help to pull Del out from under us." Bass' support is qualified, though. "Maybe you can blame a lot on him," he adds, before saying, "But if we were doing our jobs as players, he'd still have his job."

In any event, that was it for Dad for managing. He finished up his career in baseball with a few years of scouting for Oakland and Detroit and then retired in 1986, ready to spend time on his grandchildren and his golf game. And for a while, well more than a decade, that's exactly how it went.

4

The Easy Way, the Hard Way

"Youth, which is forgiven everything, forgives itself nothing; age, which forgives itself everything, is forgiven nothing."
—George Bernard Shaw, *Man and Superman*

IN MY YOUTH, WHAT FEW SKILLS I had in baseball I acquired effortlessly, mostly through play. A little pepper with Luis Aparicio and Nellie Fox does wonders for a nine-year-old's skill with the glove, especially when the glove is a hand-me-down from Luis himself. Many of my best-remembered moments from my childhood center on these things: those pepper games in Comiskey, a photo session in Fenway with my older brother and my father, and many, many more.

In Charleston, West Virginia, where Dad managed the Senators in 1960 and I was the batboy, I recall the team flew out of Charleston's airport on a well-aged DC-3 from Purdue Aeronautics. Dad wouldn't let me fly with the team because he was afraid the plane might go down and while he had to be on it I most certainly did not. The loss of that plane would have ended a promising future for the Minnesota Twins, by the way, since the heart of Dad's lineup became the core of the World Series Twins team of 1965.

That same year the pepper games were with Zoilo Versalles and Don

Mincher and Jim Kaat and other soon-to-be big-leaguers. I felt somehow like I belonged, though certainly they all were just being nice to the manager's son. Six years later, the spring of my freshman year of college, I encountered most of them again when I came to Orlando's Tinker Field to spend a few days with Dad at the Twins' spring-training camp. I'd just finished spring football practice at the University of Minnesota, where I was a scholarship quarterback and tight end. I planned on joining the U's freshman baseball team in a few days, so Dad, who was using those excellent fungo skills of his to help out where he could with the big-leaguers, arranged for me to be at first base as he hit a couple of dozen groundballs to Versalles at shortstop. On the first ball Versalles charged the easy grounder, gloved it smoothly and made a cross-body throw to me at first.

And it scared the hell out of me. The ball came with such velocity that I had a hard time getting the mitt on it and worried for my health. I was too proud, or too stupid, to admit my fear and so I stayed out there for another twenty minutes and managed to not get hurt mostly because Versalles (who died in the mid–1990s) recognized my weakness, remembered me from simpler days in Charleston, and so took something off the ball. Never once, to my relief, did he throw a ball that I had to dig out on the short hop or otherwise make any kind of tricky play on.

I remember that late-morning workout so vividly because it was a turning point in my life: I wasn't good enough, not even close, to play at that level and felt with despair that I never would, or could, be. Hard work, perhaps, might have remedied that, but hard work was not something I was then interested in and Dad, bless his fatherly heart, catered to my weakness. Within a month or two I'd quit the football and baseball teams at the U. (though I was told by the coaches I showed promise for both), transferred to a junior college in the sunshine in Bradenton, Florida, and changed my life: in some ways for the better, no doubt.

Truth is, I'd never really learned to work hard at anything in life until my time spent as a caregiver. Football and baseball and basketball came easy to me. Academic studies: easy. Career: let it just happen, take it easy. Raising my Down syndrome son hasn't been work, it's been a joy, and the same with my daughter and my twenty-three years of marriage to a wise and patient wife. Effortless.

This sense of an easy life was a factor in my struggle with caregiving, since taking care of Dad and Mom was most certainly not effortless, nor easy. It was damn hard work, mostly unpleasant, mostly stressful and always challenging. It was an ongoing battle between my goals, which centered on love, duty and honor; and my reality, which centered on my cowardly desire to just quit, to just cut and run and dump it on someone else.

For all of my faults in the caregiving task, though, I didn't do that; I didn't quit, I didn't run, I didn't walk away and phone it in. I was there. I did the job and tried to smile as I told the necessary lies to my parents and, sometimes, to myself. Caregiving asked a lot of me and I'd like to think I responded reasonably well to the challenge, at least externally. Looking back with the wisdom of hindsight, I wish that I'd gotten more help sooner, emotional help and guidance mostly. It was, I quickly discovered, the emotional challenges that are the hardest ones. But, foolishly, I toughed it out, thinking I had to. It is only in the writing of this book that I've discovered how much help I might have received had I only known where to look for it.

Had I searched for advice then as I did in the months after Dad died, I would have found a world of help from several different directions. The American Association for Retired Persons (AARP), for instance, has a very helpful on-line area devoted to the very issues that pressed upon me (http://www.aarp.org/families/caregiving/). Had I only had the courage and humility to seek help there and elsewhere on the Internet I would have found articles like "Boomers Become Caregivers," which discussed the stress and strain of the sandwich generation, and articles like "Taking Care Without Taking Over," and "Balancing Work and Caregiving" and "Factsheet: Caregiving and Depression" and many more.

AARP says there are more than twenty million baby boomers out there trying to do our best for our elderly parents. An official study of the phenomenon that you can find on that AARP website has the headline, "Squeezed, but Not Stressed."* This study says many of us are doing just fine handling things, though it notes that four out of ten of us have both sides of the sandwich, with children under 21 as well as living parents, the result of boomers starting families late and the elderly living longer. In my case, there was the soccer-playing daughter, the Down syndrome son, and the two parents, each with his or her own list of problems.

The "Squeezed but Not Stressed" study notes that we boomers are, generally, "comfortable with our responsibilities." Then, a few paragraphs later,

*A national survey conducted for AARP by Belden Russonello & Steward and Research/ Strategy Management. Xenia Montenegro, Ph.D., Knowledge Management Project Manager, July 2001.

it adds ominously that there are what it calls "A few cracks in family relationships."

It says, "Some [boomers] are beginning to feel the strain of having elderly parents, young children or both. Most pressed are those with direct responsibility for the care of their parents and other older family members. Almost 20 percent report stress generated by the care needs of the older and younger family members." Well, count me in that 20 percent (which comes to some four million of us, by the way). Count me, too, in the 46 percent of boomers who transported an older relative to the doctor (nearly ten million of us), the 36 percent who talked to the doctors (about seven million of us), and on and on.

The study makes it sound like a whole lot of us were pretty busy and pretty stressed out by our duties. And sure enough, when my friends and I talk about our parents these days the conversation often turns to how hard the job is, trying to give them a final portion of their lives that's imbued with respect and care. It worries us, we admit, when we think about our own aging. Will we put these pressures on our children? Will I act toward my daughter and son as my father acted toward me? God, I hope not.

In many cases the stories I hear from my friends sound an awful lot like mine—unhappy and demanding parents, harried and frazzled adult children doing their best for them often while raising their own kids at the same time. Misunderstandings and trying times all around.

There are differences here and there between what I read about caring for elderly parents and what I found with my own. The literature focuses on helping your parents be as independent as possible and the entire aging industry is geared toward that, trying to offer a sense of self control and self sufficiency while also meeting the needs of the elderly. I know my mother-in-law, in her early 80s now and widowed for some years, remains adamantly on her own. She lives in her own home, maintains her circle of friends, walks her dog, helps keep an eye on my son. Her one concession has been, wisely, to give up on driving at night. Otherwise, she is like millions of people her age, determined to do things on her own and maintain control of her life.

I'd like to think my own mother would be doing these things, too, if dementia hadn't stolen her mind. As it is, my siblings and I have done our best to take care of Mom with the dignity she deserves and the lies she needs to hear to get through each brand-new day. One sister sees her several times a week. I see her every few weeks. When I talk with her, she thinks she's just arrived for a Florida vacation, and that's fine with me. If she doesn't remember today that her husband of nearly sixty years died a few years ago, that's fine, too. I've learned to go with the flow. She's safe and she seems content. One of the sad-but-true realities of Alzheimer's is how its victims lose the ability to recognize their own limitations. Loved ones and children and friends fret more over the victim's decline than the patient herself, once the progression reaches a certain, inevitable, point.

Mom's dementia in its early stages was especially hard on Dad in his final year, throwing another issue at him on top of all his physical ailments and his emotional struggles. For most of his life he'd counted on her and then, unhappily, he had to be in charge. All the daily decisions were his, and he didn't like that very much. Unlike most of the elderly people I've read about, he was disinterested in independence and preferred, instead, the adulatory dependence he'd spent a lifetime getting comfortable with. He wanted, and expected, all the help he could get; from his wife, from me, and from everyone else.

It took his physical therapists a few sessions to figure this out. Most of the elderly men they work with do not want to be pampered and are offended when a therapist seems even slightly condescending. Their pride is at stake and so these men try hard. But Dad's pride operated differently. He wanted the therapy to be done *for* him, in what I think can only be a reflection of his lifetime in baseball, where traveling secretaries handled the business details and a devoted baseball wife handled the kids: all he had to do was keep playing or coaching with a bat and a ball and humbly sign his name to various cards, caps and scorecards.

A good example of this was when Dad had his cataract surgery. After each eye had been worked on we took him to the ophthalmologist's office for the standard post-operative checkup. In both cases he frustrated the doctor by not making much of an effort to focus with the new, clear lens in his eye. "You have to try and focus, Mr. Wilber," the doctor had to urge in both cases and then, finally, grudgingly, Dad made the effort and sure enough, things began to come into focus for him.

Some months into his final year the therapists who worked with Dad asked me to come in and talk with them about his behavior. They worried over his lack of progress and his increasing reliance on his wheelchair when he could, if he would just try, still be walking, albeit with the help of a walker. We chatted about who Dad had been and who he was now and in an intuitive flash of insight one of the therapists realized that the mistake she was making was in being too nice, too supportive. Del Wilber didn't need a helping hand, she realized, Del Wilber needed a stern coach, someone who would demand that he give it some real effort. She said she'd give that a try and in a few days Dad was doing better, up on his feet and using the walker to make it from one end of the room to the other, listening all the while to the therapist as she demanded from him "One more step, Mr. Wilber, one more step."

On the day Dad and Mom arrived at Tampa International Airport I was there to meet them, waiting at the gate, smiling, excited, as they walked toward me. I'd been to St. Louis to see them just a few weeks before, thinking at the time that I was making my last visit with my dying father.

In St. Louis I'd found two surprises, one of them really welcome, the other more worrisome. First, for a dying man Dad was looking pretty good. It turned out that my sister Mary, who'd lived near Dad and Mom and visited them often for many years, had done battle with the physician who'd taken on Dad's case at the nursing home and she'd won and so Dad was not only alive but improving. The doctor had planned to let Del Wilber die in peace, his time run out. Mary, who'd done her homework, knew that in cases like Dad's the drug Lupron often proved effective. The doctor recommended against this, but Mary talked to a family friend who's an excellent physician and when he agreed with her she insisted on the doctors trying Lupron on Dad's prostate cancer. The Lupron worked and in days Dad began to improve. When I arrived it had been a week or so since the drug had been administered and Dad insisted he was feeling good. I didn't believe him, not yet knowing about Lupron or its effectiveness. He continued to insist and I continued to disbelieve, until I talked with Mary and she explained to me how Lupron wins a reprieve for some lucky men. Dad, as it happened, was one of the lucky ones and was, as he said, feeling pretty damn good.

There was no question about it at all: Mary had saved his life. After I returned home to St. Petersburg and my computer I finally did my own homework on Lupron and found that its effects were usually temporary. In a few months or perhaps a few years, Darwin's inexorable logic would kick in and the cancer cells would figure out the Lupron and overwhelm it. But for now the drug had brought Dad a welcome respite and he looked good—amazingly good, actually—as he walked out of the jetway and over toward me. He was using a walker and moving along pretty good with it. I was impressed.

Mom, too, was full of surprises; less happy ones, as it happened. I'd noticed during my St. Louis visit that she seemed distracted and confused. I put it off to her age and the tiring demands of her role as Dad's wife. Since Dad had gone from the emergency room to the nursing home she'd been making the ten-mile drive from the family home in Kirkwood to the nursing home almost every day to spend time with him. The emotional and physical demands of that daily task seemed to be taking their toll. She seemed confused and forgetful, and she had a strange twitch or spasm that would strike her every now and then. I wasn't too worried, and figured it was mostly stress. I told my sister we would get her to my favorite doctor in St. Petersburg, a hard-working family-practice physician and a friend. He, I said, would figure out what to do about these things.

At the airport, she came walking out from the jetway with an attitude I'd first noticed during my St. Louis visit: a jaunty, cocky stride, full of confidence, a woman with attitude. She smiled when she saw me, waved heartily and said, "Florida!" to me.

"Yep," I said, and gave her a hug. "Welcome to the Sunshine State."

Taffy (her nickname for as long as I can recall) had always loved Florida. She loved the beach and the sand and the sunshine and even the humidity. After Skip (our father's family nickname, derived from the baseball jargon for a manager) retired, she made sure they spent a few weeks in the St. Petersburg or Naples area just about every year. My well-traveled older brother would use his frequent-flyer miles to get them plane tickets and they would spend the time in one nice hotel or another in St. Pete Beach or, even better as far as they were concerned, they would stay at older brother's second home in Naples, where Dad would play golf and Mom would sit in the sunshine, visit the shops, or go with family or friends to one waterfront restaurant or another.

Mom had acquired her love for Florida during her year visits from 1946 to the early 1960s for spring training. In those better days she'd been both mom and teacher to us. Nearly every spring of my childhood I'd left Mary, Queen of Peace School in suburban St. Louis and headed south to Florida in late February for spring training. There, usually in a rented house at the beach, I spent the mornings with my brothers and sisters, the older ones with our workbooks from school, being what we would now call homeschooled by Mom. She'd had one semester of college, at the University of Texas, but she put what education she had to the test by teaching two and then three of us our lessons. As I recall we always came back ahead of the rest of the class: and full of memories from Indian Rocks Beach or Pass-a-Grille or Clearwater Beach or, when dad was managing in the minors, the cooler but still happy times in Fernandina Beach in the northeast corner of Florida.

After Dad retired we all tried to convince him to move to Florida. We certainly had Mom's full support, but getting the old ex–Cardinal to leave St. Louis—that most baseball of cities—seemed an impossible task. He had a circle of admirers he met for breakfast in downtown Kirkwood most mornings, he spoke at Kiwanis and Optimist meetings, he was interviewed on KMOX and he was mentioned now and again in broadcasts and he was, generally, the old pro in a baseball town. He was well-liked and respected and he loved it there, no surprise. Only when Death knocked on his door did he change his mind, and even then it was half-hearted as he tried, I think, to do the right thing for his wife.

But they did finally move to the sunshine and the heat where, the plan was, Mom could enjoy the Florida she'd wanted for so many years and Dad could enjoy being taken care of by the wife he loved. It just didn't work out quite the way we'd planned, that's all.

5

Writing Dad

I AM A MINOR-LEAGUE STORYTELLER; like my father, I'm a journeyman. I am, I suppose, a second-rate novelist who's still trying to learn that craft; but I do a decent job, I think, at the short-story form where I've enjoyed some success. I think of myself as downright passable at essays, too, and I also write feature stories and reviews, and labor hard to write useful college textbooks. I've even had a few dozen poems published in respectable magazines and anthologies and some of them, I'd like to think, weren't too bad. I don't win awards with my writing but generally I get it all published, sometimes by good publishers and often in good magazines or newspapers. I am not a critics' darling nor do I make a lot of money at it, but seeing my work in print pleases me and knowing there are readers who get something from what I have to say affords me a certain sense of self-worth. In my teaching, as in my writing, I am often entertaining if not particularly knowledgeable. As a result, I get mostly good student evaluations; this is because entertainment, to an undergraduate, out-hits knowledge every time.

And so for thirty years as a teacher and for forty as a writer I've been telling stories of one kind or another, some of them as true as I could make them and others pure fiction. I began writing professionally while I was in college, working as a sportswriter for the *Bradenton* (FL) *Herald* and then the *Metro-East Journal* in East St. Louis, Illinois. By the time I'd graduated I was writing bigger, arguably better, sports stories for *Sport Magazine*, *Football Digest* and others.

51

Then I started graduate school and teaching, and at about the same time I left sports writing, which I'd come to find boring and repetitive, and started writing fiction. I'd always been a heavy reader of science-fiction and fantasy magazines and novels, and so that was the genre that most appealed to me as a writer. In a few years, after the usual rejections and tribulations, I began to sell some of those stories even as I was diving deeper into the academic ocean, teaching journalism at schools like Southern Illinois–Edwardsville, (then) Mankato State University, Florida Southern College and then the University of South Florida, where I've now been for nearly twenty years, introducing hundreds of students at a time to the promise and perils of the mass media in large lecture classes or working more closely in smaller classes with beginning and advanced reporting students as they work to learn a few things and get a head start on the craft and art of journalism. I'd like to think I've had a positive impact on some careers.

In my writing I have talked about my father from time to time. Some of these stories were the truth as I know it, others were fictional and based only loosely on Dad and his career. Looking back over the body of work that touched upon Dad I can see some telling ironies. Some of the fiction has been more truthful than I knew it to be when I wrote it; some of the non-fiction, on the other hand, has proven to be, regrettably, less truthful than I'd sought. I now think of all this father-son oriented writing as BC (Before Caregiving) and AC (After Caregiving), the experience of taking care of Dad having altered the way I view my writing, myself, my father, and the relationship between those three elements.

On the fiction side of my writing, the BC stories include a pretty good short story from 1997 called "Where Garagiola Waits," which first appeared in a magazine called *Fantasy & Science Fiction* and has been reprinted elsewhere. I'm at work now on the novel-length version of that story, which follows an elderly ex-ballplayer as he goes to a nursing home to visit his wife, who suffers from Alzheimer's. It's February in St. Louis as the story starts, and the wife, in her dementia, thinks it's 1946 and that her newly-wed husband has come to take her along to spring training, where he's been given a chance to make the Cardinals after his war years. To humor her, the ballplayer takes her for a little drive that matures into a trip to St. Petersburg along those old highways heading south as her dementia somehow twists and bends their shared memories of better days into an odd sort of new reality where hope and dreams and baseball mingle as they travel along.

The story is about addiction and dementia and baseball and love and redemption. I wrote it years before I came to realize the truths that I now see in it: Mom's and Dad's struggles with alcohol and nicotine and our family's addiction to a romanticized version of baseball that trapped us in an ambered past, catching us mid-stride as we rounded second base and making, I think, Dad's final days much tougher than they needed to be.

In another BC short story, "Run Down West," I invented the death of an elderly one-time big-league catcher who'd let a passed ball get by him in a World Series game. The narrator of the story, a surviving son, comes home to a small town in Illinois to bury his father and to try and bury, as well, some tragic memories. I wrote this story, too, long before Dad's health problems surfaced, and I showed it to him before it went into print, searching for some approval from him. He read it and said he liked it all right but that he was worried that people might think he'd had a passed ball in a World Series game. To please him I put a disclaimer at the front of the story talking about how facts are altered to turn them into fiction and mentioning that Del Wilber never had a passed ball in a World Series game. (Dad, in fact, was never in a Series game, barely missing the opportunity on three different times when he was with the Cardinals, the Phillies and the White Sox.)

In other short stories from that BC era I continued to invent other father-son relationships, always using my father as the starting point for a fictional creation and using me and my brothers or wholly fictional creations as the son. The technique seemed to work, though I suspect a reader going through all those stories at once would find things dismayingly repetitive. Happily, I didn't limit myself to father-son relationships in my short fiction and a broader view of the forty or so published stories would show at least some variety in theme, setting and characters. But there was a bone there, I think, and I gnawed at it. A lot.

In non-fiction I wrote a number of essays in which Dad figured one way or another. Some of those were for one of my favorite little magazines, *Elysian Fields Quarterly*, a very good literary review that focuses its interest on baseball and publishes some of the best baseball fiction and non-fiction to be found anywhere. Others were for newspapers, several of them for the *Tampa Tribune* and one for the *Boston Globe Sunday Magazine*.

For the *Tribune*, I wrote several pieces on my own return to baseball after years away from the game. By the time I turned thirty, a lifetime of immersion in the game had worn me out and I drifted away, no longer playing town ball with a local team or even paying any attention as a fan. Then,

in the 1990s a convergence of things brought me back. First, I began playing catch in the driveway with my wife, a pre–Title IX athlete whose frustrations with the lack of sports opportunities for girls in her era hadn't
pushed her so far away from an athletic life that she couldn't find a way to
enjoy playing soccer in a co-ed adult league in Winter Haven, Florida, or
enjoying a game of catch with her husband. The purely physical joy of playing catch again called to me, I had to admit.

Then I began to cheer on the city officials in our home town of St.
Petersburg who were struggling to acquire a major-league team. Their hard
work finally paid off in the start-up of the Devil Rays in 1998. At about the
same time I listened to the urgings of my wife. Tired, perhaps, of wasting
too many evenings throwing a ball back and forth with me, she convinced
me to go to a practice for a local over–40 team, the St. Petersburg Cubs.

I went and I was hooked, and so at an age when wiser men are fishing
or playing golf I became again an infielder for a baseball team. I wrote
about that return in several pieces for the *Tribune*, talking a bit about my
family history and Dad's role in the game and also about the physical joy
I found (and still find) in acts as simple as hitting a baseball or fielding a
groundball.

I also wrote in those articles for the *Tribune* about an unanticipated
benefit from my playing ball for the Cubs: it gave me something to talk about
with my father. He wasn't interested in my writing or teaching, beyond
politely reading a story or two in which a character based on him appeared.
And I'd spent too many years ignoring the game he'd made a life of and so
I couldn't coherently discuss the latest trades or the merits of one particular player over another. We didn't have much to say to each other, Dad and
me.

Every now and then during that long inadvertent estrangement I'd try
and reach out to him and even then I would usually get it wrong. When my
wife and I saw the film *Field of Dreams*, I found myself deeply moved by
the movie's interest in the odd love triangle formed by fathers and sons and
baseball. I called him to tell him I'd seen the movie and was affected by it.
I called to tell him that I loved him. The phone call embarrassed him. "It's
just a game," he told me that day, and he added "It's just a business."

Ah, well.

The peak of my BC writing was a story I wrote for the *Boston Globe
Sunday Magazine* in 1998. Dad had encountered the start of his health troubles with a fall in the front yard that broke a wrist and then some lower back

troubles finally diagnosed as spondylosis, a degenerative narrowing of the spinal canal. In a few months he went from gardening and the occasional round of golf to walking with a cane, then a walker, and finally into a wheelchair. In the story I talk about how he urged me on in my youth even when things weren't going great, and how I tried to pay him back now that he'd encountered these physical challenges. The story tells the truth as I knew it at the time, but I couldn't see the future and the deeper, darker troubles to come. I'm not to be blamed for my optimism, I suppose, but the benefits of hindsight help me see my own limitations as a writer in that story.

When we brought Dad and Mom to Florida I embraced with pride and considerable energy (at least at first) the caregiving role. I'd get to know Dad at last, I thought. We'd build a relationship. I'd pay him back for the terrific childhood I'd enjoyed. It would be good.

But it wasn't good, or even close. Within weeks I had to face the hard truth that the relationship we were building was a painful and, maybe, destructive one, and that I didn't like getting to know this particular version of Dad.

I wrote about this in what I think of as my first AC piece, an essay for *Elysian Fields* written in August of that year. I wrote for the first time about the difficulties of caregiving for an old pro of modest talent but considerable pride. I started with the story of Dad's special day in Philadelphia when he hit three homeruns in three at-bats and so created a family myth that sticks with us all to this day. I focused on the realities of caregiving; on its necessary challenges and its frustrations. That essay and several more ultimately grew to become this book, which has occupied my non-fiction writing time for more than three years now, at the expense of a major textbook that I should be working on and a novel that needs one more revision.

While writing this memoir I got an e-mail from an old student from years ago, now a good friend and a fine editor. Did I have a new short story or essay I could contribute to his magazine? I did, of course; I had a dozen of them from this book, but I didn't want to steal something directly from this effort and, instead, wanted to come up with a new contribution, a story that thought through the theme of this memoir while writing something safely fictional about caregiving, about myself, my father and mother, my family and, mostly, about the struggle we all will finally face with death. That story, "Prices," appeared in early 2006 in *Gulf Stream*, the literary magazine of Florida International University.

I'd like to think I treated Dad, and his memory, with honor in all of these stories and in this book. The truth holds its own kind of honor, for starters, and lies, no matter how well intentioned, their own kind of dishonor. Del Wilber was a child-man as he struggled to deal with the terrible challenges that come with facing death. I was his son, and as much a part of his problems as his solutions, and so I, too, struggled to get through those hard times. I'd like to think that the effort made me a better person for having gone through it. I'd like to think that I learned some valuable things about debts and payments, about children and adults and adult children and childlike adults. I'd like to think that it reinforced my sense of obligation to do for others what needs to be done, as the Jesuits had taught me, as my Down syndrome son has taught me. And I'd like to think that the experience taught me, too, about mediocrity, and time, and honor, and where I fit into all that, and where Dad fit in, too.

6

Using Dad

I'M AT MY DAUGHTER'S JUNIOR-VARSITY soccer game, cheering for her as I've cheered for years as she's gone through the complex levels of modern American youth soccer, from micro-soccer as a six-year-old when her mom and I coached and where you don't keep score, to local recreational soccer where the competitive aspects are downplayed and the concentration is on fundamentals, to more serious levels of the game where the best (or most interested, or most moneyed) of the recreational players join together to play other serious teams from other serious towns, and on to select soccer, where the best few from various town teams join together and the financial, travel and practice demands—as well as the competitive nature of the game— increase, sometimes dramatically.

All these levels of youth soccer have degraded the middle-school and high-school value of the game, which is a shame. Many of the girls and boys on the select club squads have participated in organized, year-round soccer for much of their childhood and so their level of play is superior to the kids who lead more ordinary lives and who have now, in seventh or eighth or ninth or tenth grade, decided to play for their school. My daughter is in eighth-grade now and yet she's playing for the high-school junior varsity. Next year, in ninth-grade, she'll be a varsity player and perhaps a starter. This strikes me as vaguely wrong in several ways, but there it is and here I am. Cheering for her is a welcome part of the deal, a payoff for the all the car drives to all those practices and games and tournaments hundreds of miles away;

and for all the money spent on sign-up fees and uniforms and shin guards and balls and water jugs and gasoline and hotel rooms and more.

My girl is a defender and a good one. I'm standing next to another dad, and he's cheering on his daughter, too; a gifted forward named Nikki who has a lot of raw talent but hasn't had the training. She's a nice kid, a friend of my daughter's, and I like her. Her father seems like a nice person, too, though we haven't talked much. Today, at this game, we're side by side and we need each other: I want his daughter to score and put us ahead; he wants my daughter to defend well and stop the other team, a local powerhouse that our smaller school always struggles against.

It's October and he's wearing a Red Sox cap. It's 2004 and the Sox are in the playoffs. We live in Yankee Country and so his wearing a Red Sox cap makes him a marked man, but on this warm and sunny day I'm in a t-shirt, blue, with Red Sox across the front. We're simpatico.

"Got to win tonight with Schilling on the mound," he says at halftime. Our soccer team is losing 2–0, but our daughters have played well so we're feeling pretty good at the moment. His daughter had two good shots on goal, one hit the upright and bounced out, on the other the keeper made a nice play to stop it. My daughter blocked a sure goal off a corner kick and cleared it, and then later used her good speed to chase down a forward who'd broken free on the far side and ended a scoring threat with a nice slide tackle. We're proud dads, despite the score.

"Yeah," I say, pausing to think about the Red Sox situation which I should know exactly. I should know who's pitching and the batting order and the defensive line-up. I should certainly know who's on the mound tonight and who's in relief and how the bullpen looks and that Curt Schilling has some tendon troubles and all of that.

But I don't.

My father's years with the Red Sox were good ones for him and for his family. The friendships he made there, most importantly the friendship with Ted Williams, would matter to Dad significantly some twenty years later. Two of those years were even pretty good for Dad statistically. In 1952 he was traded by Philadelphia to Boston after appearing in just two games for the Phillies. In Boston that season he appeared in forty-seven games and hit a respectable .267. Then in 1953 he was mostly a pinch-hitter, appearing in fifty-eight games, with one hundred twelve at-bats and twenty-seven runs-batted-in with just twenty-five hits, for a .241 average. That was the season where he had more runs-batted-in than hits and earned his way into that elite group of players with more runs-batted-in than hits for the season.

The Red Sox years were good to me personally. I was four, five and six years old and I was the son of the Red Sox pinch-hitter. I was too young to realize quite what that really meant and I'd been raised as a son of the Phillies' catcher and the Havana Leones' catcher and the Rochester Red Wings catcher and so I was too deeply immersed in baseball to really realize that most of America's children weren't, in fact, allowed to roam around the outfield in Fenway on a sunny summer day, trying to be just like my talented older brother, he of the strong arm and the good glove and the powerful swing.

But I wasn't too young to know the summers were long and golden in Boston. Mom, always Mom, took my brother and sister and I on outings and I have memories of guns firing in mock battle at Concord Bridge and of the first time I saw the Old North Church and recited portions of what must have been one of the very first poems I learned, Longfellow's "The Midnight Ride of Paul Revere." Hardly a man is now alive/ Who remembers that famous day and year. Indeed.

To the best of my recollection I enjoyed just about every moment of my three summers in Boston, including time in the clubhouse in Fenway, where I must have been underfoot and in the way of Jimmy Piersall and Hoot Evers and Ellis Kinder and Dom DiMaggio and the Splendid Splinter himself, in the way that the sons and daughters of many of today's players are in the way in the clubhouses of today's millionaires.

I loved it there. It was an important part of a happy childhood. Dad was someone I knew well in those days, and I loved and admired him. My father-son experience with Dad on the day he arranged for me and my older brother to have our pictures taken in Fenway is the most complete single-day memory I have from anytime in my life before sixth or seventh grade, and it is a memory that can only happen in a childhood so blessed that one's father was a major-leaguer. I wrote about this day once for a story I did for *Elysian Fields Quarterly*. In that article I talked about how I remember walking onto the field at Fenway with my older brother and Dad. We each wore our uniforms, Dad in his familiar number 33, my brother Del Jr. in his number ½, and myself in my number ⅓. George Woodruff was the photographer, using a large camera with a bellows: probably a Graflex.

As I remember it, the shoot had originally been planned for just Dad and my older brother, who'd recently been given a very official-looking Red

Del Wilber, Red Sox catcher, instructs son Del Jr. (center) and the author.

Sox uniform. But I'd been as envious as you might imagine a five-year-old to be, and I'd thrown a fit in the back of the old Pontiac when I heard the news. My mother—bless her heart—scrambled madly to include me in the goings-on. She cobbled together a uniform for me from my brother's old child-sized Havana uniform, the one he'd had when Dad spent his season of winter ball in Havana in 1950. To make the uniform work she took a Red Sox decal—the ones with the half-crossed red socks—and sewed it over the heart. Somewhere, too, she found me baseball pants to fit. They were loose, but then all the pants were loose in those days, even for the big leaguers.

I already had a glove—a hand-me-down from one of the Red Sox players that was much too big for me, though I don't remember being concerned about that; and I wore, I think, my trusty Converse All-Star shoes. You can see the picture on page 61 in this book. Dad is watching me cross first base,

Safe in Fenway, the author touches first base in 1953. At right is Del Wilber, Jr., and behind is Del Wilber, Red Sox catcher and pinch-hitter.

my brother is stretching out to make a catch of the ball being thrown by someone off-camera.

It was all posed, of course, frozen moments where we stood there for the photographer and pretended to be playing the game. But posed or not, this set of pictures is among my most precious belongings.

It was Dad, and it was the Red Sox, and it was Boston, and all the difficult times to come, those last months when I tried so hard but so ineptly to take care of Dad in the midst of his pain and anger and disappointment were far, far away, in some distant, less-happy future.

The month before my parental soccer game discussion, I'd been in Boston for the world science-fiction convention, the annual gathering where many thousands of fans, writers, editors, movie-makers and more come together to celebrate the genre. I could have called and tried for free tickets to a Red Sox game while I was there, I suppose, but it didn't seem right anymore, and so I contented myself with just walking down to Fenway with a friend, Martha Soukup, a marvelous science-fiction writer and a friend who shares a sort of academic interest in the Sox (she's a Cubs fan, to be honest). We walked the two miles from our hotel down to Fenway, enjoying every minute of the stroll down Boylston until the ballpark slowly came into view and we crossed a parking lot and we were there.

Scalpers wanted to sell us tickets, but they were asking $100 for standing room and that was well out of our price range, even for Fenway in September. Had we known how it was going to work out for the Sox that year we might have thought differently, but that was in the future and unknowable, even for a pair of science-fiction writers.

I did walk into the Souvenir Store on Yawkey Way and bought a Red Sox cap and a t-shirt, so I had tangible proof that I'd been there. Just those two things set me back nearly forty dollars, which is certainly a comment on modern baseball. The game, in a delicious bit of synchronicity, was against the Rangers, the team Dad managed for one game in 1973.

Ten years before I'd been at another convention in Boston and back in those BC days I'd still thought of myself as part of baseball's family, so I'd called dad to see if he could get me tickets to the game. I hadn't been in Fenway since 1954.

He took care of it, called me back with a phone number, and when I dialed that number, sure enough, two tickets were waiting for me. I grabbed a colleague and we went to see the game. The flood of memories on that day was rich and thick, the smells of the place, the feel of the seats, even the I-beam that blocked my view of right field: all of that was Fenway and it was 1954 and I was six years old in Boston and Dad was down there in the bullpen warming up Frank Sullivan or Sid Hudson. All of those memories came back that day. I don't remember who the Sox were playing, or their place in the standings, or much about the game at all. What I remember is the smell of beer and peanuts, the sound of the crowd settling in and then coming awake at key moments, the feel of the steel girder and the hard slats of the seats. It was all a kind of time machine, a science-fictional day, something from *The Twilight Zone*, yanking me back forty years in a heartbeat.

My recollections of those days and dozens more flashed through my mind in an instant or two when I stood there next to Nikki's dad and tried to take part in his Red Sox conversation: should I tell him about my time spent running around on the grass in front of the dugout while the Sox took batting practice? Should I mention that Ted and my dad were pretty good friends? Should I talk about leaning back against that left-field wall and looking up to a blue sky and realizing, even at age five, that this was something special?

Or should I just shut up and honor my commitment to walk away from the game that I now associated with pain as much as with pleasure? Wouldn't it be wrong to use Dad like that? Hadn't I promised myself not do that anymore? I hadn't played the game, after all; it had been Dad who'd done that. Wasn't it time, at last, to grow up and live my own damn life and not my father's, to quit conjuring him up from the grave just to brag about a youthful moment or two from a half-century before? Hell, I hadn't even really paid any attention to the Sox. I knew they were playing well but only in the last few days had it finally occurred to me that they were in post-season play, against the Angels I read in the paper; and then, if that went well, they'd play the hated Yankees.

I struggled to say something lucid, based on the newspaper I'd read that morning. "Yeah," I said, "but that ankle...." And I let the thought trail off knowingly.

"I hear he's going to get it stapled or stitched or something and keep pitching," he said, "and then get surgery in the post-season."

"Pretty risky," I said. "What's his paycheck?"

"Twelve million bucks. But he wants to win this year."

"So he's going to risk that ankle?" I marveled in admiration.

A month later I felt differently about Schilling. It had to do with politics. He'd spoken up for George W. Bush and against John Kerry, though Kerry was a Massachusetts senator and a long-time Red Sox fan and an athlete to boot, still playing hockey from time to time. Still, on ABC's *Good Morning America* show, Schilling said near the end of an interview, "Make sure you tell everybody to vote, and vote Bush next week."

A secretary in the academic department where I teach had read that quote and liked it. Like many of the staff and faculty, she's a Republican. She sent me a happy note on it, rubbing it in. I'm a Democrat and I responded to her with an ill-considered e-mail that asked why anyone should pay the slightest bit of attention to the political musings of a Red Sox pitcher?

Schilling's comment was just one more nail in the coffin of my baseball interest at the time. Too much angry old man. Too many demands over too many months. Too much attention paid to minor memories from the major leagues (and, perhaps, not enough paid to major memories from the minors). Too much, really, all the way around when it came to baseball and ballplayers and opinions. And so I'd sworn off my interest in the national pastime. I was done with the game. I didn't want to talk about it. I didn't want to talk about Dad's small part in its history. I didn't want myself connected to all that.

But the month before all that, I stood there with Nikki's dad the Red Sox fan and thought about whether or not to drop Dad's name. I'd been telling myself I didn't care about baseball anymore and that I saw too many dark connections between the man I'd known at the end of his times and the man my father had been in his prime.

Still, he'd hit some important pinch-hit home runs for the Sox. He'd caught Mel Parnell. He'd been friends with Ted and George Kell and Hoot Evers. He'd played in Fenway for three years and I'd played there, too, in my own way. I have memories of that. I have pictures. It really happened.

My wife knows how I wrestle with all of this and she knows me better than just about anyone. She was watching and listening and smiling as I talked baseball with Nikki's dad. Would I drop the dad bomb into this conversation after all? Hadn't I finally grown up enough to not see the need for that?

I hadn't. I did. I glanced at my wife and smiled and shrugged my shoulders. "You know," I said to Nikki's dad, "my father played for the Red Sox. He was a catcher. In the 50s."

His eyes grew wide, he leaned my way to hear more, and we were off and running.

7

Special Needs

I HAVE A DOWN SYNDROME SON, Richard Wilber, Jr. He's a remarkable young man and I've written about him often in published essays and short stories. He's been working at the same McDonald's for a dozen years, he lives in his own apartment, he has an active social life with other special people. He calls all this "My good life."

But, of course, it's all a kind of fabrication. His life is protected, with special coaches helping all along the way and with myself and my relatives sheltering him and protecting him so he thinks he's a lot more independent than he really is. Once a week or so he and I play one-on-one basketball. He wins every game 15–14. I could play hard defense and keep him scoreless, and if I chose to drive the lane he wouldn't be able to stop me. I could win every game 15–0, but what would be the point of that? I would rightly feel worthless for having done it, and he might no longer want to play the game that has given him so much joy and done him so much good.

Instead, my feeling is that life has given him enough losses; so when Richard Jr. plays basketball with me he always wins, and it's always close and it's always fun, ending in sweaty hugs and high-fives. I give basketball a lot of credit for his success in life. The game has taught him that when you work hard and practice you can accomplish something: in his case the accomplishment begins with his sweet jump shot from about eighteen feet out and his good sense for the game and then goes on from there to more important things like his good health and his love for exercise and even the friends he's made playing the game. There's a very talented local player named Nick—a teenager blessed with size, speed and shooting skills—who's become a friend of my son's and often joins us to play. It's amazing to watch the two of them—the talented six-foot-four playground star and, next to him, my son—shoot around and joke and play. Just two young guys shooting hoops.

In the things I've written about my son, like those I've written about my father, I've used Richard Jr. as the starting point for some fictional character with special needs who meets Sir Lancelot in Scotland, suffers at the hands of a warped bad guy in Florida, or meets a ghostly grandfather in a baseball game, or helps a troubled uncle in a shopping mall. I use these characters in stories because they're useful and interesting and even fiction writers tend to write at least in part about what they know.

Every now and then I write about the real Richard Jr.; my son, the Down syndrome child who's grown to be a man; a very, very good man. My favorite of these short essays ran in *Catholic Digest* magazine a few years ago. It's short and, I'd like to think, a pretty good piece of work, just like my son.

SUMMER RULES*

Scattered dark clouds threaten rain, but it's a Sunday afternoon and for me and my boy that means time for the weekly game. I have enough writing deadlines to get me near panic, but I ordered my priorities twenty-three years ago when the boy's mom left us, and I stick with them. Hoops it is.

We grab the ball from the garage floor where it's cornered by the Radio Flyer and his red Huffy bike and walk out toward the driveway and the street beyond to take the one-block walk to the courts in the small park I can see from my office window.

We walk over the road's culvert that connects one canal to another in our island neighborhood. A young guy and his wife, out for a ride on their expensive bicycles, straddle their bikes on the north side, watching the water emerge from the culvert's opening.

I know them vaguely as neighbors, I've seen them drive by in their Volvo, all smiles and friendly and perfect. Things aren't cheap here, the young couples that can afford to buy into this neighborhood now have made their money early. We have a lot of lawyers and young doctors and commercial airline pilots and their stay-at-home wives. This is a nice, safe place to raise a couple of kids.

Twenty yards farther out the canal widens into Boca Ciega Bay, and from there to huge Tampa Bay and then out into the open Gulf. Right where they stand, though, the water is narrow, confined to an orderly flow.

*Catholic Digest, *April 1998. Reprinted with permission of Bayard Publishing.*

"What you see in there?" my son asks them.

"Saw a coconut float in that end," the guy says, pointing to the other side of the road, "and we're waiting to see it come out this side. But I think the tide changed or something right while it was in there."

"I check," my boy says, and hustles over to the south side. He likes to be helpful. There, cautiously, he leans over to look down. He has a bit of a height thing. He can do it, can stand on high places and look out to see what's there. But he doesn't much like it, he's a lot more comfortable down where things are solid and straightforward and dependable.

Now, though, he manages to lean over a bit and take a look, his curiosity overcoming his fear. "No. I see nothing," he says, and stands back up straight, proud of himself. "I sorry for you," he adds pleasantly, and backs away from the edge. The couple just smile at him.

We walk on, my boy in front leading the way, dribbling the basketball, alternating his right and left hands as he sends it down to the cracked pavement and stops it on its way back up to send it down again and again. He's something of a master at this, at walking along, holding the dribble.

My boy has Down syndrome. In a week he'll be twenty-eight. He's put on weight in recent years, but he's still in pretty good shape for a Down's kid. He plays basketball and does his fair share of walking. He holds down a good job at McDonald's, too, flipping burgers and cleaning the place. Twenty hours a week. He's been there five years. I'm proud of him beyond speaking.

We get to the courts and loosen up. I miss a few from fifteen feet, and then back up a step or two and hit, count 'em, six in a row from the three-point line. The rim enlarges, becomes a huge, wide open canyon for me, and the ball just drops through time after time while my boy feeds me.

"Wow, you a hot man, my dad," he says. And then I miss one, and then another, and he laughs. I laugh with him. These things never last.

He takes a few shots, misses them all badly, and then comes in for a lay-up. He misses that, too, the ball rimming out.

He shakes his head, walks over to the head of the key, does his favorite little turn-around move, and launches one from eighteen feet. Swish.

I feed him and he hits six of the next eight, five of them clean swishes that hiss as they go through the netting. "I on fire," he says with delight, and I couldn't agree more.

We decide to play just one game today, to fifteen by ones, switch, take it back, call your own fouls, win by one. We both know the jargon, we're both intimate with this game. Once, years ago in St. Louis before we moved down here to the beach and the heat and the summer showers that come early some years in April, I watched him play in a Special Olympics game against a team of high-functioning kids that should, by rights, have blown my boy's team out.

But the kid was in his zone, as they might say today. He hit two jumpers, a couple of those turn-arounds, stole the ball once and raced the length for a lay-up, and went on like that for the whole game. His team lost, but only by six points. My boy had eighteen of his team's twenty-two points. At game's end, exhausted, he sat on the court floor while every single player from both teams came over to shake his hand. On the sidelines, watching, I cried.

His mother left us when he was five years old. A new boyfriend, a big motorcycle, some excitement, and no more having to deal with disappointment. I'd thought we had a pretty good marriage going until that day she was late picking me up at the university. When she came by in the Volksie van things were strangely tense until we got home. Even our boy, in the back seat, just sat there, quiet, his eyes wide. Later on, I figured out what he'd seen.

A few weeks later, after the initial shock of her leaving had gone numb for the two of us, I sat my boy down and told him I'd be there. Always. He told me the same thing and we shook on it.

God knows I've screwed some things up since then, but never that. I said always, and for him that means right to the end, whenever that comes. The experts figure all Down's kids will get Alzheimer's. They also figure most will be dead by the time they're fifty or so.

Me, I'm no expert, but they also told me, way back then, that'd he'd never read, never hold a job, never amount to much at all. An institution, they said, would be best. Now, when he reads me the Cub scores or looks at the movie ads, I allow myself to remember those days and I smile.

We start our game and he opens up a quick four–nothing lead, hitting three outside jumpers and a lay-up. I'm ice cold, missing everything, and badly.

I finally make one, a banked-in jumper from the wing, and then he answers with a turn-around to make it five–one.

As he hits that shot the sun comes out and at the same time it starts to rain. In a surreal tiny downpour that must have started on its way down while the cloud was in just the right spot, we continue playing, the rain hissing into a low cloud of steam on the hot court as the sun bakes it off.

We don't stop. Our summer rules are that we play no matter what, unless there's lightning, and this weather is so like summer that we count it as July, not April.

He hits a few more and then he misses one badly as I finally get hot, hitting from outside, draining three in a row from that spot on the wing, climbing back into the game until I tie it at eight-all.

We trade baskets a couple of times, both of us shooting well in the warm rain and bright sun. Then the rain eases to a drizzle, then to a mist, and the sun dries the court so fast that the only wet spots are those in the shadows from the basketball standard, where there's an arced wet spot that comes out toward the free-throw line. It's a little slick there and we have to be careful of our footing. It's not a problem for him, really, since he'd rather shoot from outside anyway. He loves the sense of drama you get from taking that long shot.

Me, I like to drive across the lane and come under the basket for a reverse lay-up, but the slick spot scares me. I'm old enough now to be cautious, so I hang around the perimeter, taking what I can get.

It's ten-all, then he runs off another streak and gets up by four. I play a little harder on defense, I don't want it to end this way.

He takes a long jumper and clangs it. I get the rebound, back out, launch a bomb from out there and get it to rattle in and it's fourteen–eleven.

He misses again and I make it fourteen–twelve. I'm talking all the time now, doing a play-by-play, trying to add to the excitement. "Now here comes Dad, trying to get back into this thing. He fakes a move to his left, pulls up for a jumper, and ... hits it! And now it's fourteen–thirteen and Rich is rattled, you can sense it folks, the kid is really rattled."

"I not rattled," he tells me, "I a good player." He flips me the ball to check it. I flip it back and he starts his dribble to the right, switches left, does a complete three-sixty spin and lets a runner go. It rims out.

I get the rebound, take it back to the line, turn and let it fly. Swish.

I go nuts. "It's fourteen-all folks, and this is a thriller. Next basket wins and you have to figure it's Dad who'll get it. The momentum has switched. You can feel the tension as Rich grabs the ball and walks back to the line to put it in play.

"He dribbles to his right. Nothing there, Dad is playing great defense. He knows this boy's weaknesses. He knows he loves to go to his right and hit that runner.

"Rich comes back to the middle. Nothing there. He backs up, backs up again. He's way outside his range now, folks. No one could hit one from there."

And he looks at me. He smiles. "I like it," he says, and he brings the ball up with his right hand, cradles it on the side with the left, brings the elbows down and then brings them back up, pushes with his arms and then the wrists and launches it, a good two steps behind the three-point line.

I turn to watch it go, arcing through the steam and the thinning mist and the sunshine, arcing right through all the special schools and the amoxicillin and the missing mom and the kids poking fun and the trouble with speech and with reading and with math. It arcs through all of that and finds its way home, rattling off the rim a bit, then settling through for the game winner.

It's the NCAAs and the NBA Finals all wrapped up into this weekly exquisite moment. He dances with joy, his arms in the air.

"Yes," he shouts, then "Yes!"

He runs over to give me a hug. I congratulate him on winning the Big One and hug him back. His sweaty face is filled with a huge grin.

For twenty years we've been doing this, the two of us.

But now I have to go. He's going to stay behind and shoot some more, just for practice, just for the joy of playing the game, of being *able* to play the game. But I have these deadlines.

On the way back I look for that coconut, checking the north side and then the south. Nothing there, so the thing must be trapped in the middle somewhere. Behind me, as I walk to the house, I can hear my boy playing, the ball against the drying pavement, the moment of silence as he must be picking up the dribble and taking the shot and then, I can hear it as I walk away, the swish as the ball goes cleanly through the cords.

My father, to his great credit, loved my son, right from the start. Early on it's easy to love a Down syndrome child: they are cute and affectionate, if slow to reach their various milestones, walking at two in my son's case, and talking at three. But love and attitude make up very nicely for slow progress, and my son loved his grandpa Skip and that love was handsomely returned, no question about it. Their mutual love started with my son's birth and continued, unalloyed, right to the end. Even in the worst of times during Dad's last months, if I brought my son along Dad's mood would brighten, his attitude would change, his hostility melt away in that big hug and wet kiss from his grandson. Rich could make Dad happy.

But I worried some over that. I didn't want to use my special son to fix my problems with my father. I didn't want to somehow put pressure on Rich that he didn't need to have. He'd managed to carve out a great life for himself despite what the experts had told me any number of times over the years, and I wasn't about to spoil that for him. So I tried to ease off on the visits with him, tried to back off on the expectations Dad had that Rich would come see him a lot. I thought I needed to protect my son.

And Rich proved me wrong, as he has so many times over the years. His sheltered apartment wasn't far from Mom and Dad's assisted-living facility and he loves to go for walks that prove his independence. So he started walking to Dad and Mom, visiting with his grandparents on his own. If I wouldn't take him, he'd just take himself.

I got the message, and returned to taking him by there often. And he kept up his own visits, too, so he was usually there several times a week, brightening up a darkened pair of lives, bringing smiles to his dour grandpa's face and softening the frenetic anger of his grandma.

He's a very special guy, Richard Jr., and I'm both enormously proud of him and deeply appreciative of his strengths and talents. I've learned a lot from him over the years, including the real truth about winning and losing, about sports and life, and most importantly about fathers and sons.

8

Assisted Living

AT FIRST BLUSH, YOU'D SAY the Wilber children don't seem to have much trouble with addictions. The five of us are lifetime non-smokers and moderate drinkers; no one gambles excessively, no one seems to be involved with cocaine or methamphetamine or heroin or anything much worse than the occasional glass of wine or, in my case, a welcome pint of Guinness or two in certain favorite pubs in the West of Ireland.

But we are the children of parents with dependencies, starting with alcohol and cigarettes and moving on from there to more subtle things. We have inherited from them at least the basics of addiction, the needs that mark it, the wanting that defines it, the enabling of it that comes from family. These needs, these wants, these enablings are hard to discover and harder to be shed of. I know this to be true, at least in my case. And Dad's. And Mom's.

During the first months of their stay in The Fountains at Boca Ciega Bay Mom and Dad lived in an eleventh-floor two-bedroom apartment. The idea in an assisted-living facility like The Fountains is that the residents can enjoy as much independence as they're willing and able to, while having their needs met by the staff when those needs arise. These assisted-living facilities are so common they've earned the acronym ALFs, and their popularity is understandable as America's elderly population grows disproportionately to the overall population.

In my parents' case their apartment wasn't large, especially when compared to the home in suburban St. Louis where they'd raised five children and then presided over a very empty nest since the early 1970s. But Dad had just spent the better part of a month mostly lying on his back in a bed at a nursing home in St. Louis, waiting to die. Now that the Lupron had temporarily brought him back to better health the two-bedroom apartment had to be looking pretty good: and the staff, the nurses and therapists and aides, were exactly what the doctor ordered as far as Dad was concerned. He'd spent his life living in hotels and he considered the Fountains just another place with a good front desk. As he got increasingly comfortable he began calling down to the reception area with one demand or another. Eventually he was calling so often and making so many demands that the facility called me to ask if I could get Dad to back off a bit on the phone calls.

For Mom, the assisted-living facility turned out to be exactly the right place for her, but for all the wrong reasons. The Fountains, like all good ALFs, offers a wide variety of activities for its residents. There is a small theater in the building that shows classic films several times a day. There is a piano in the main lobby where professionals and amateurs take turns at the keyboard. There is a large meeting room where everything from exercise classes to motivational speeches take place. It's a very full list every single day of the year, and I had figured on Mom taking full advantage of these offerings. There is a shuttle bus, too, that runs to the local malls and a public transit "trolley" (it's a propane-fueled bus dressed up to look like an antique trolley) that stops out front every half-hour or so and goes to the nearby beaches and to the surprisingly lively downtown St. Petersburg.

Surely, I had reasoned, Mom would be on that bus and heading west to the beaches or east to downtown several times a week. She had always been active, even in retirement, running her own local cable television show for the senior citizens of St. Louis County, and writing and editing for the tabloid newspaper the senior-citizen center published regularly. Before that, she'd worked in public relations for hospitals and before that she'd worked in promotions for the Cardinals front office. She also helped create the Pinch-hitters, the Cardinal charity organization comprised of current and past baseball wives, and she'd been a radio reporter and had her own radio show on KMOX in its glory days as the clear-channel flagship radio station for the Cardinals and St. Louis' other sports teams. During all of this she'd raised us; all five of the children mostly a product of her hard work and love since Dad was often out of town. She could, she did, do it all.

But now we discovered that that particular Taffy Wilber wasn't around anymore. Instead, the new Taffy Wilber was limited by the terrible changes in her mind: changes brought on by a combination of various health issues, but mostly by the initial stages of Alzheimer's, that implacable enemy of the self that we came to know so well and with such sadness. This new Taffy Wilber wasn't as capable as the previous one. This new Taffy couldn't remember directions or lists or, as time progressed, quite where she was. This new Taffy was sometimes angry and often confused, but still loved to talk, and for months she and Dad enjoyed eating in the main restaurant of The Fountains, a clean and large room where meals came on good china with silverware and an attentive wait-staff. She even made friends with some of the other residents.

But even as she did these things I could see we were losing her and that she was in the act of becoming someone new. The terrible struggle between the old Mom we'd known and the new Mom who was emerging from the rubble of the old one's collapse was difficult to watch. Dad, no surprise, greeted the changes with disbelief. Our father was like a lot of men from his generation (or, my wife would argue, men from any generation). He was addicted to helplessness when it came to housework and other family matters. Like most men of his era, he was disinterested in the dishwasher, the ironing board, the PTA, the high-school vice-principal, the terrifying eighth-grade nun at the ironically named Mary, Queen of Peace School, the helping with the music lessons or the difficult math homework or the worries about sex that struck around age fourteen: all these and more he left up to his wife and our mother, who handled them pretty damn well, at least as far as I'm aware. Dad felt his responsibility was to be a baseball man: first as a player and then as a coach or manager or a scout. His role was to be a part of the national pastime, to be a friend of the stars of his generation and a teacher to the stars of the next two or three generations, to be known as a nice guy among his peers, to be a storyteller and a wage-earner. His job, as far as I knew in my childhood, was to stand near the batting cage and lean on a bat.

His only cooking was outdoor on the grill or, when inside in the winter, in large amounts on the stove-top, bubbling up a very good pot of chili or soup, a skill he'd acquired a certain expertise in when he managed in the minor leagues and found himself, as minor-league managers often do, to be not only the boss of the team's on-field efforts but also the hands-on cook for a couple of dozen hungry young men who were getting paid very little to live their dreams.

Dad had been babied and protected as a child. Then, with hardly any time at all after high school to find any sense of adulthood or independence, he'd found himself a part of baseball's family, where he prospered as a person if not always as a ballplayer, playing and coaching the game for the military during the war or, after, playing or managing or coaching or scouting for forty more years in big-league and minor-league cities all over the country.

He'd been pampered as an infant and as a child and then pampered still more by living in that sort of Peter Pan version of adulthood that professional athletes enjoy. His father and mother, the military, baseball's traveling secretaries and the games noteworthy lifelong friendships, his beautiful wife and his adoring children: all had a hand in creating his addiction to dependency. After a lifetime of being waited on and catered to, the hard

realities of his final years, when things spun out of control on him and the only person he could call on, literally, happened to be me, he did the only thing he knew how to do: demand to be taken care of, demand to be pampered as he'd been for decades. Trouble was, I wasn't very good at the role he saw me in. And so we struggled.

Mom's addictions were more typical. Dad told me with pride how he'd introduced her to cigarettes when they'd started dating and how glamorous she'd looked as she'd smoked. He didn't tell me he'd introduced her to alcohol, but I suspect that was the case. I know from his letters to her during

Taffy Wilber, radio journalist for KMOX in St. Louis, interviews Joe Namath at Busch Stadium.

the war years that he was struggling with his drinking even then. In one letter I have that he wrote to her during his time in the military he promised to get his drinking under control. He didn't keep that promise, really, until some fifty years later.

Over the years, Mom lived two, or maybe three, separate lives. Early on she was the perfect baseball wife; blond and beautiful and with one cute kid after another. Later, by the 1960s, she was a career woman, in radio and then the Cardinal front office and then, after that, in public relations. It was a stressful, demanding lifestyle for her as she balanced her career with her obligations to her children. She mostly did a pretty good job of it, but eventually she paid a sad price and was hospitalized in the late 1970s for a breakdown and then again in the 1980s for the same thing.

She had left St. Louis before the first of those breakdowns, working for a friend in hospital public relations in Miami. I happened to be visiting there (using it mostly as an excuse for a spring trip to Florida) and she had just been hospitalized when I arrived. I was mystified by it all, clueless as to her struggles and the reasons for her collapse. She recovered and returned to St. Louis and resumed her life, slowly working her way back into public-relations work before collapsing again. It was then we began to hear about her troubles with alcohol. Dad was part of that, an enabler for her addictions as he'd been since they'd met in San Antonio forty years before. A doctor and friend, a brilliant guy they both liked and admired, told them both they had to quit, get off the booze and get cleaned up or face more of these struggles. My sister Mary told Dad, especially, that he had to quit or Mom wouldn't be able to. To their great credit, they *did* quit, Mom joining AA and Dad quitting his drinking in support of her. It was, I think, one of his finer acts as a husband.

By then Dad had retired from baseball, his final years of scouting pretty listless anyway, friends keeping him in the game in one way or another as he played out the string of a long, mildly successful career punctuated by those few notable achievements here and there and those several excellent years of minor-league managing.

So together, he and Mom shed some of their worst addictions during the late 1980s throughout much of the 1990s, and in doing so they entered a kind of golden retirement, Dad playing with the grandchildren and working endlessly on crossword puzzles; Mom, cautiously I think, beginning her new career in the media as a semi-retired editor and writer, handling both that local newspaper for seniors and the cable television show for the

St. Louis County older residents program. Mom even quit the smoking habit Dad had helped her start in 1943, though switching the habit from cigarettes to nicotine gum didn't turn out the way any of us would have chosen.

We all enjoyed this golden decade. Dad had a very warm-hearted seventieth birthday party in 1989: Stan Musial and Marty Marion and other ballplayers of his era were in attendance, and my sister Mary put together an amazing scrapbook filled with good wishes from everyone from Brooks Robinson and Joe Garagiola to Ted Williams and dozens more. At that party I read a poem I'd written for the occasion. In the late 1980s I'd visited The Baseball Hall of Fame in Cooperstown and I remember finding his name mentioned in there, not as a member, of course, but in the minor-league section for being, I think, a manager for the Pacific Coast League All-star game in 1974. I mentioned that obliquely in the poem, and only all these years later do I realize what that mention must have sounded like to Musial, a player who'd earned his way into the Hall through his career-long excellence. Stan, I hoped, laughed at my hubris.

That poem and a whole sequence of baseball short stories I wrote through the decade of the nineties point to my own addiction; one I'm working to wean myself from. Hello, my name is Rick and I've been addicted to the myth of baseball.

Dad and Mom's golden decade began to play out by the late 1990s. First Dad slipped while trimming bushes in the front yard and broke a wrist. Then he struggled with spinal stenosis. Then came hip-replacement surgery and the realization, during the preparatory work for that, that he had prostate cancer. By the time he'd rallied (if temporarily) from the cancer and we'd brought him down to Florida he was also in a struggle with Parkinson's and nearly blind from cataracts. Helping him try to respond to all of these challenges and even worse ones to come, like the lung cancer and the congestive heart that ultimately claimed him, fell mostly to me and to my sister, Mary. We did our best.

9

The Aristocracy

POOR DAD. THE FIRST TIME I saw him raise that arm I knew that he—and so me, too—were going to have some trouble.

We were at my daughter's soccer game, ten-year-old girls already dropped into the cauldron of competitive sports, playing hard, playing with determination, no frilly girls allowed: the Pinellas FC Under-11 girls against the mighty New Tampa Comets.

His recovery had never been complete from the hip replacement surgery that came after a nasty fall in the front garden of the family home in suburban St. Louis, and so that evening I figured out how to park our van alongside the field where his granddaughter was playing so Dad and Mom could watch without having to get out of the van. I slid open the side door for Mom and rolled down the front window for Dad, and then I got out to stand next to where they both sat so we could talk and watch and cheer.

Near the end of the game I walked away for a few minutes to see the action at the far end of the field and when I turned to look back and check on them I could see Dad opening that front door and trying to stand.

This was no small feat. The Parkinson's, the prostate cancer, the artificial hip: these things conspired against him, so opening the door, turning in the front seat of the van to get his feet out over the pavement, getting them down to firm ground, pulling on the door handle and the side-frame to tug himself forward and up at the same time was an achievement, an act of courage, of defiance. He *would* stand, and so he did.

I stopped and watched for a second, impressed. Then I turned back to see how my daughter was doing, her team clinging to a 1–0 lead.

I heard Dad clear his throat behind me. I turned to look, and he was standing erect, holding his right arm up in the air and slightly forward. He didn't say a word, but cleared his throat again—haarrumph.

I didn't get it, that first time. What did that mean, that raised arm?

He stared at me.

"Yes?" I asked. "What's up?"

He stared. He was wearing the red St. Louis Cardinals jacket that one of his daughters had bought him as a gift. He liked the jacket a lot and wore it often.

"I don't understand," I said, and raised my shoulders.

"Well," he said, "it's getting warm."

"Yeah, nice isn't it?" I said.

"Well," he said, but I was turning away. Here came those Comets again. My daughter moved forward, took the ball off the toe of the Comets right-winger before the girl could shoot. My daughter dribbled to her left, used a toe pull to get past the other girl, moved back to the right and sent the ball shooting down the field. It was a heckuva move. I couldn't help it, "Yeah, Sammy. Great play!" I yelled.

She glanced at me. She frowned. Shut up, dad. I could read it in her body language. I shut up.

A life in baseball teaches certain lucky and talented men that childhood games are forever and that, as baseball players, they comprise, for many Americans, a kind of aristocracy.

My father was a back-up catcher. Never a star, he enjoyed his few singular moments of success in the game, like the day in Philadelphia when he hit those three homeruns or the May in Boston when he hit back-to-back pinch-hit homeruns in separate games.

The result of these and a few other similar moments was that even in his eighties he received mail weekly asking for his autograph. Fans sent baseball cards and other artifacts for him to sign; they asked questions about his favorite players from his era; they wanted to mine his memories of that golden age in the national pastime. I helped him with those, typing up his answers, helping him sign the cards. My secretarial skills are solid though I could never hit a curveball. In my life I had to give up any serious play with the glove and the ball and the bat and, like most men, grow up.

78

There was more throat clearing behind me. I turned. That arm was still raised. "Sun's out now," he said.

"Yeah," I agreed, still not getting it.

"Well," he said, "It's pretty warm to be wearing this jacket."

Ohhhh. It dawned on me at last. I walked over and helped him take off the jacket. He sat back down afterward, tired from the exertion. In front of him, the game ended. We won. There was a happy granddaughter who walked our way, sweaty and dirty and smiling. There was a smile, too, on Dad's face; a rare thing to see. "Way to go," he told her. "You played great."

"Thanks," she said, and then got busy with her post-game snack—chocolate chip cookies and Hi-C.

After the soccer game I dropped Dad and Mom off at their assisted-living facility and then rejoined my wife and daughter at our house, nearby. After our daughter showered in both water and praise, we dropped her off at a friend's house to play, then we went to see a movie, the first one I'd seen since my parents had arrived in town.

The film, *Gosford Park*, is director Robert Altman's penetrating look at the foolishness and condescension of the British aristocracy in the last years of the old empire. There is a scene in there where the Countess of Trentham—played perfectly by Maggie Smith—sits at a mirror, preparing herself for a formal dinner. Her servant, Mary—played by Kelly MacDonald—stands behind her as the Countess raises her left arm straight out to her side, talking of nothing, simply raising the arm.

Mary understands instantly, and steps forward to put bracelets on that raised arm.

Later in the movie Mary hears from Mrs. Wilson—played by Helen Mirren—as Wilson describes herself as the perfect servant because she not only responds well to her Lord's needs, she can anticipate them. She knows what he will need before he knows it himself.

I watched as she said that and I thought of my father, and of baseball, and of how the game affects at least some of the men who played it in the major leagues. And I thought of those fans who write to my father still. And I thought of that that arm he raised for me.

10

Myth and History

THROUGH ALL OF DAD'S AND Mom's troubles, our family myths about them grew and enlarged even as their reality narrowed and became more confining. For Del Wilber's sons, especially, the mythology of baseball became increasingly important as he declined, in a way that seemed to be a directly-inverse proportional response to his various illnesses. This is understandable, in that we wanted to remember him in stronger, happier, better days. But as the months passed this familial baseball folklore grew like Jack's beanstalk until it towered over us and overwhelmed reality. Later, when my hard-earned new realities had forced me to confront the myths, this new perspective led to considerable friction between me and my brothers, and especially between me and my younger brother, whose memories included warm baseball summers as a batboy in various minor-league cities where Dad was the manager.

Dad's daughters, my sisters, had always had a less romanticized view of Dad and Mom and the lives they'd led. My sisters had seen and understood the good and the bad. For Del Wilber's sons, though—and I include myself in this—the myth of baseball outweighed any realities we didn't want to know about. For us, baseball—and, by extension, Dad—was viewed through a soft-focus lens that added green grass and Georgia clay and sunny, blue-sky days to everything Dad had been or tried to be. I'm convinced that this myth of baseball that we created wound up causing Dad some unhappiness in those final months as he tried hard to live up to our expectations.

80

As my own understanding of Dad and Mom developed, I slowly came to realize that growing up inside baseball gives one a skewed version of reality that must be similar to that held by the children of Hollywood stars (from "B" movies if the analogy to Dad's baseball career is to hold) and of politicians or other public figures. We were a special family and we knew it. When your mother wakes you up early each year on a late February morning to get you moving so the family can start the long drive south to spring training, from slush to warm sand in a two-day drive, you do get a sense of being special. When your father's friends have nicknames the sportswriters have given them like The Splendid Splinter and Stan the Man and your friends are the children of those friends of your father's, you can't help but acquire a certain sense of your elite status, whether or not that status really exists or is in any way deserved. This status we enjoyed was an accident of birth, but we certainly didn't think of it that way; it was, for all of us, a fact of life, often a blessing and occasionally a curse.

I recently read Deeanne Westbrook's very interesting book, *Ground Rules: Baseball & Myth*, which talks at length about baseball and mythology. To read her book is to begin to understand how this particular game has acquired its status in literature and cinema. Reading chapters about "Baseball and the Classic Monomyth," or "Fathers and Sons, Blessings, and Baseball's Myth of Atonement," or "Baseball's Historical Bricolage: Borrowed and Stolen," helped me understand not only how baseball has co-opted any number of archetypes from Western literature, but, more importantly, how everything from Mark Harris' *Bang the Drum Slowly* to Bernard Malamud's *The Natural* to W.P. Kinsella's *Shoeless Joe* and many more standards of baseball literature and film fit rather neatly into our culture's standard way of perceiving plot, character, setting, theme, metaphor, symbolism: the whole palette, in fact, of good storytelling.

Westbrook points out that there are really just two archetypal plots: "Someone went on a long journey," and "A stranger came to town." Think it through a bit and you'll see that every work of baseball art or literature fits into one or the other of those. The game itself, in fact, folds nicely into one or both, from the annual arrival of the strangers in town each spring in Florida or Arizona, to the long journey of each season and the mythic quest that Henry Aaron and Frodo Baggins and Stan Musial and Odysseus and Babe Ruth and Harry Potter and Lou Gehrig and Mr. Pickwick and Barry Bonds and Huck Finn all go on.

For the Wilber children, Dad was part of that quest, both annually for various teams and, over his lifetime, professionally: searching throughout much of his career for the Holy Grail of a big-league managing job.

That's a path, a route, a voyage, that all athletes pursue; some with more success than others, some with more joy than others, some more happily than others. It's a voyage that exacts a toll, from the player and from his or her family. It's a voyage that brings joy and, sometimes, sorrow.

Where Westbrook talks about fathers and sons I read with special interest how the literatures of baseball present "a stunning contrast in their depiction of mothers and fathers." The fathers, she notes, are often worshipped as heroes, as in Mark Harris' *The Southpaw*, where son Henry says, "I always carried Pop's glove, and I was proud to do it.... It had that leathery oily smell of which is 1 of the best smells I know,"* or, most famously, in *Shoeless Joe*, where the ghostly father's wishes are the motivations that move the entire story forward.

As in *Shoeless Joe*, the death of the baseball father is typical in these mythology-based stories, and that death usually includes the father giving his blessing to his son. At that point, notes Westbrook, "The son ... is compelled to take up the father's work, work in which the father has labored but in the performance of which he has fallen short, or to take on the task of redeeming the father through the telling of his story."†

I read that and I think of our family and I realize how this mythological connection to baseball resonates for us, especially for my brothers and me. After Dad's death, my younger brother, the one who hadn't been able to visit Dad very much during that final year but had called him often, sent around an e-mail detailing the dream he'd had the first night after Dad's death. In that dream Dad had visited him, told him what a fine son he was, and conferred that blessing. My brother needed that blessing, obviously. I could have used one, too, I suppose, but contented myself with my feelings of relief that the emotional turmoil had (I thought) come to an end.

Since Dad's death I've received a string of e-mails from my older brother, relating one pleasant encounter after another he's had with men who knew and liked our father. These men all have stories to tell, usually of what a nice guy Del Wilber was or how he helped them along in the game in one way or another. My brother, obviously, keeps Dad's memories, the best of them anyway, alive and well by seeking out these stories and sharing them with us all.

*Deeanne Westbrook, Ground Rules: Baseball and Myth *(Champaign: University of Illinois Press, 1996), p. 255.*
†*Westbrook, Ground Rules, p. 260.*

Myself, I have a rounder view of Dad, I think; one where the wonders of our childhood are tempered by the hard times at the end. But I, too, am clearly trying to carry on the baseball myth even as I dispute its merits. I'm writing about it right now, in fact, in the hope that my growing understanding of Dad and his family and our place in the game will prove interesting and useful for others. Maybe it will. Maybe I'll strike out.

The amazing thing about our family's enjoyment of the baseball myth was that it was mostly based on a pleasantly mediocre career. It wasn't so much what he'd done that made Del Wilber important, as who he'd known. In some cases he'd had a real impact as a coach or manager, especially in the minor leagues where he was, several times, a pennant winner. But most of his later career as a manager and scout was reflective of his earlier performance as a player: he was a journeyman, he was a routine laborer in the business of baseball. Yet we made much of this; more of it, quite possibly, than it deserved, and in so doing we trapped our father — and, some of us trap him still in our memory of him — in a myth of our own creation, a myth of reflected glory that, for better or worse, we continue to tell to anyone who will listen.

To this day, not only my older brother's e-mails but most of our shared sibling e-mails talk about Dad and nearly always start and end with some baseball memory; someone from the St. Louis area, perhaps, that one of us met and who remembered Dad telling one great story or another at a banquet dinner or spinning tales over breakfast with his admirers at his favorite diner in suburban Kirkwood, Missouri. Always it's baseball. Other than medical-crisis e-mails during the final months of Dad's life, I don't recall a single e-mail from either brother in reference to our father that hasn't used baseball as the avenue for the discussion. We don't know any other way to talk about Dad, which is amazing when you think of it. What do sons of fathers who were ironworkers or dentists or teachers or firefighters talk about when they speak of their father? Is it all work related or do other, more personal things, get into the conversation? My brothers and I don't seem to have any idea how that might work.

With my sisters it's different; they remember a different father from the one who raised their brothers. But for my brothers and myself, we created a mythic father figure and, perhaps, by doing so we caged him. This was a sad thing we did, catering to his self-image in a way that encouraged his dependence on a past that really hadn't happened quite that way.

Judith Viorst talks about these family myths in her very fine book *Necessary Losses: The Loves, Illusions, Dependencies, and Impossible Expectations That All of Us Have to Give Up in Order to Grow*, a book I'll talk about later in more depth. When she talks about myth she notes that all families have built up their own myths, and that "these family myths will not have uniform impact on all of its members. We each will respond in our own individual way. But if they are powerful and insistent, [they] are going to have to be reckoned with someday."* And reckoning with our family's myth, obviously, is at least partly what this book that you are reading is about. Viorst adds that there is a very real pressure for family members to adhere to the myth, since "We feel guilt about our negative feelings.... And what we may do to defend against, or alleviate, our guilt is to loudly insist that the person who died was perfect. Idealization—'My wife was a saint,' 'My father was wiser than Solomon'—allows us to keep our thoughts pure and to keep guilt at bay. It is also a way of repaying the dead, of making restitution, for all of the bad we have done—or imagined we've done—to them."† Yep, that sounds like us; "perfect idealization" all the way, with the national pastime and its heavy load of history and mythology tossed into the mix, too.

This idealization is not limited to Del Wilber and his wife and children, of course, it's part of our culture's obsession with baseball and especially with the game in its golden age from the late 1940s to the late 1950s, before the Dodgers and Giants moved to the West. In his important and accurate book *Past Time: Baseball as History*, author Jules Tygiel talks about what he calls "this idealized view" of baseball from that era, and focuses a few pages, by way of example, on what is arguably baseball's most famous moment: Bobby Thomson's "Shot Heard 'Round the World" off Ralph Branca on October 3, 1951.

In 1951, Tygiel notes, "The game ... seemed, both figuratively and literally, closer to the fans than later editions. Baseball still maintained the limited geographical configuration established a half-century earlier. Ten cities, none further south or west than St. Louis, hosted sixteen teams. Teams played in stadiums largely built in the teens and early twenties, located amid urban neighborhoods, within walking distance or streetcar or subway rides of most fans. The ballparks, most which, like Ebbets Field, held between

*Viorst, Necessary Losses *(New York: Free Press, 1986; reprint, 2002)*, p. 224.
†Viorst, Necessary Losses, *p. 242.*

30,000 to 40,000 fans, brought fans close to the action. The players themselves were less remote and more accessible. Bobby Thomson and Ralph Branca, the two pivotal figures ... epitomized this link."

Tygiel adds that the "two memorable artifacts of Thomson's shot have left the game indelibly etched on the nation's soul. The first is the remaining newsreel footage of the game, showing Branca's pitch, Thomson's swing, and Thomson exuberantly romping around the bases, stomping on home plate into the jubilant arms of his Giant teammates. The second is a recording of the Giants' radio announcer Russ Hodges's famous home run call:

"Branca throws again ... there's a long fly ... it's gonna be ... I believe ... the Giants win the pennant ... the Giants win the pennant ... the Giants win the pennant ... the Giants win the pennant."

I play the Hodges broadcast in a large introduction-to-media class that I teach. In the section on the history of radio news I share several famous broadcasts, including the impassioned description of the Hindenburg disaster by WLS announcer Herb Morrison, several of Edward R. Murrow's live-from-London broadcasts during the Blitz in the first years of World War II, and others. The Hodges broadcast, an excited voice speaking directly from baseball's golden age, deserves inclusion and is, to my mind, in radio's all-time top ten for most memorable broadcast news snippets.

But here's the truth: not many people actually heard Hodges on that October day in 1951. As Tygiel explains, "Only a small proportion of those experiencing the game did so via Hodges's broadcast.... In New York City the playoffs were broadcast by Hodges and Ernie Harwell on WMCA, the Giant station, while Red Barber and twenty-three-year-old Vin Scully handled the Dodger accounts on WMGM." The game was also broadcast nationally (and available in New York City) on the Mutual Network with Al Helfer, a former Dodger and Giant announcer. In addition, the game was televised on Channel 11, the Giant station, with Hodges and Harwell alternating between radio and television. While still a new medium, television was popular in New York City and many, perhaps most, homes had a receiving set. Television sets were already established as standard in New York's bars and grills, as well, and many New Yorkers watched the game in those establishments.

Also, the use of the newsreel footage of Thomson hitting the ball, the reaction of the fans, and then Thomson rounding the bases is almost always used in conjunction with the radio broadcast, though they were, of course, utterly separate media and only later combined into one of baseball's best-loved moments from history.

Ironically, not only were there relatively few fans listening to Hodges' broadcast, there were no formal recordings made of any of the broadcasts of that era, and it was only through a fluke that a Dodger fan, Lawrence Goldberg, happened to use an early tape recorder to capture the final inning of what he thought would be a Dodger victory. Goldberg called Hodges the following day and offered him the tape, and the famous broadcast, saved by a thoughtful fan of the opposing team, over time was conflated with the newsreel footage to assume its stature.*

Most fans, even those alive at the time, have altered their reality to suit their memory. But baseball is as much about statistical accuracy as it is about mythology and there are nearly as many of these corrective stories about the game's myths as there are members of SABR (the Society for American Baseball Research), who spend no small amount of effort keeping track of the game's realities as well as its legends. Part of the game's appeal, after all, is its sense of history, leading to reasonably valid comparisons of today's players with those from twenty, fifty, eighty or one hundred years ago. Corrective stories can be found on such famous events as Enos Slaughter's "Mad Dash" (no, Johnny Pesky didn't hold the ball)†; Fidel Castro's famous tryout with the Yankees (never happened)‡; and many more. Baseball, no surprise, has been inventive with its history; or perhaps it is better to say that those who remember and cherish the game sometimes embellish their memories, leaving others the task of finding the truth hidden in the invention.

For instance, it is ironic that the late 1940s through late 1950s are remembered so fondly by baseball fans, since attendance in that era wasn't high. Tygiel points out that in 1951, after a brief post-war boom, major-league attendance sank to just over sixteen million total (down from nearly twenty million a few years before) and two years later it was down to just over fourteen million. Even in New York, only 4.3 million fans total attended the home games of the Yankees, Dodgers and Giants combined, despite the heated pennant race between the Dodgers and Giants. In fact, Tygiel notes, at the final home games for those two teams, "only 19,000 people appeared at Ebbets Field; a scant 6,000 at the Polo Grounds."

Yet in the mind of the general public baseball's greatest age was gen-

*Jules Tygiel, Past Time (New York: Oxford University Press, 2000), pp. 150–151.
†Bill Nowlin, Mr. Red Sox: The Johnny Pesky Story (Burlington, MA: Rounder, 2004), p. 96.
‡http://www.snopes.com/sports/baseball/castro.asp.

erally anytime before 1960, when men were men and smoked cigars in the stands while rooting for the Mick or Teddy Ballgame or Rapid Robert or The Iron Horse or Big (or Little) Poison or, of course, The Babe.

And this, unfortunately, is where some of us children of Del Wilber ambered our father, freezing him in mid-stride as he rounded third on his home-run trot in August of 1951 or remembering him as he dived back toward home plate to tag Yogi out in a game in 1952 or, closer to a broader reality, seeing him as the pennant-winning minor-league manager patiently waiting for his chance the big-league job.

I now look back on the father I thought I knew before I took on the care-giving role and I shake my head at my foolishness. I believed in the church of baseball, as Annie calls it with such conviction in Ron Shelton's *Bull Durham*. And I did this despite Dad's own feelings about the game. For most of his life baseball was a job, not a religion, and he scorned those who made too much of it. Baseball was a game with a ball and a stick and a glove. And, lucky him, it was a lifetime job, too; but that meant work, not play. It wasn't romantic. It wasn't fathers and sons playing catch in the back yard. For Del Wilber, baseball was filling out scouting forms or traveling in minor-league buses or spending months at a time away from home. And that was all it was. A job.

But we didn't see it that way, and we didn't want him to. For all of us in his family, all of his children and our children; there was never any question about where the focus was: Del Wilber, big-leaguer. We created this myth and we reveled in it. We lived inside it so long, in fact, that it was understandably hard to see how silly it might seem to outsiders.

I had an inkling of this during a Thanksgiving dinner we hosted during Dad's last year. His health was on the upswing about then and he very much wanted to come to the dinner with Mom and enjoy the meal and the usual adulation from family and friends. The old pro would be there and could be coaxed—if you tried hard enough—into telling you about the time he hit three home runs in one game in the second game of a doubleheader for the Phillies in August of 1951. Or the time when Jimmy Piersall, his room-mate for a time when they both played for the Red Sox, had walked and then scored without even holding a bat at the plate. Or the time when Dad posed for a Norman Rockwell cover painting, standing in for Ted Williams, who wasn't willing to spend the time needed for the cover art. Or, or, or, or ... the list, if not exactly inexhaustible, was certainly lengthy.

That was the Thanksgiving that followed the horrors in New York City on September 11, but we were giving thanks for having food to eat and iced tea to drink and for having Del Wilber around when we thought we'd lost him. It was mostly my wife's extended family in attendance. Her mother and an aunt. Her sister and that sister's grown daughters. Her brother and a friend of his. I get along well with all these people. I like and admire them. They're good, honest, hard-working, intelligent, caring people.

But they're not baseball fans. They don't care about the baseball myth. They don't know about Bobby Thomson or Big Poison or Shoeless Joe or any of the rest of it. And so, as far as they were concerned, my father was just my father and my mother just my mother. The interesting fact that he'd played a game professionally nearly fifty years before didn't mean much to them.

For a while, after we'd eaten the turkey and the mashed potatoes and the green-bean casserole and the croissants and the stuffing and the corn, we talked about what seemed to matter in November of 2001: the new war on terror, the nation's slow emotional recovery from the horrors of September 11, and more. The closest we came to a sports discussion was a few comments on the Florida Gators football fortunes and the then on-going troubles of the Tampa Bay Buccaneers.

Dad sat in his wheelchair at his usual place at the head of the table. Mostly, he was quiet, this particular conversation not holding much interest for him. He was not the focus of attention. At gatherings where my side of the family held sway he'd have been at the heart of every conversation and the talk would have been of sports and little else. He'd have had his strong opinions and no one would have argued with him. His sons and daughters would have prompted him to start in on one great story or another and he would have faked a grudging acquiescence and then the story would have rolled on out and we all would have listened. But not at this Thanksgiving. These strangers held other interests. These strangers weren't baseball fans.

After awhile I noticed him calling Mom over. Her dementia was still under diagnosis at the time and so we couldn't put a name to it, but she was often forgetful or belligerent or both; but during that Thanksgiving gathering she was on her best behavior, chatting away happily with people, doing fine conversationally, as Alzheimer's patients can do at times, especially in the disease's early stages.

Dad asked her to get something for him out of her purse and she reached in and found the prize he wanted: some hand-made baseball cards, double-sided, with a picture of Dad from his days with the Red Sox, in a

Hand-made, two-sided baseball card.

catcher's crouch, on one side and on the other side a picture of him in his Phillies uniform.

These are cards cheaply made by a well-intentioned friend of Dad and Mom's who put them together and then gave them to Dad and Mom to hand out to their friends.

I never quite understood the appeal of the cards: Dad, after all, was on plenty of legitimate baseball cards from Topps and Bowman. In front of me as I write this is a Topps 1952 Reprint Series card of Dad in his Red Sox days. He's got that baseball stare going on, his arm is cocked back ready to hurl the ball down to second and throw someone out who's trying to steal. He's wearing his catcher's chest protector but his Red Sox cap is on with the bill forward so you can see the red "B," which gives away completely that this is a posed shot. On the back it gives his statistics and says this:

"The Red Sox got Del from the Phils in May '52. The Phils drafted the experienced receiver from Rochester in '50. In '49 Del was player-manager of Houston. Besides managing the team, Del played the outfield, infield and pitched, along with his regular catching chores—he also hit .308 that season. He broke into baseball in '38, was in the Army 4 years and got his first trial in the majors with the Cards in '46. His hobby is decorating baseballs for the winning pitchers."

Pretty interesting stuff, that; but Dad and Mom didn't make copies of that card, or any of his other cards from eight years as a player. Instead, they chose to use the home-made cards, and on that Thanksgiving Day Dad handed around some of the cards for all to see and, if they wanted, keep as mementos of the time they sat down to a meal with Del Wilber, ex–major leaguer.

Ever polite, my wife's family looked at the cards, smiled, handed them around to one another, said something about how nice that was that his friend had made them for him, and then, to Dad's dismay, handed them all back to him without asking any of the standard questions: "Did you know Ted Williams? Did you win any pennants? Did you play in Yankee Stadium? Fenway? Ebbets Field?"

These are the kinds of questions that I'd learned baseball fans would immediately ask of Dad in the waiting rooms of doctors' offices or in the local Wendy's, and he'd be off and running when they did, feigning humility and reluctance until prodded a second or third time, at which point he would shrug his shoulders as if the weight of all this was almost too much to bear, and then dive into one great story or another.

In the six months I'd been his caregiver at that point, I'd seen him do this successfully dozens of times and I admit to being an accomplice. My job—and it was one I accepted too willingly—was to get the conversation rolling, which was easily done with the doctors and nurses but was a little trickier in the waiting rooms or restaurants. Still, I nearly always managed, usually by asking Dad to comment on something current in baseball ("Man, Dad, the Red Sox blew that one last night. Why did they leave the starter in?"), which forced him to reply, mentioning with reluctance the time in Fenway in 1952 when manager Lou Boudreau had done something similar.

It was an easy enough way to keep the old pro happy, but it didn't work on this Thanksgiving Day though I tried, a little embarrassed to be doing so in front of family and friends. They didn't bite. There were no questions forthcoming about old ballplayers or old games or old stadiums. There was just an uncomfortable quiet as they handed the cards around, mumbled something polite, and then gave them back. To them, these makeshift cards were just makeshift cards; cheap cardboard pictures, double-sided, like something a seventh-grader might make to show to his pals. The people in our house that day included an elderly but very active lawyer (a woman who'd gone through law school in the 1930s and 1940s, fighting her way through the male-dominated system that clearly didn't want her), a school principal, a high-tech wizard on a major corporation's fast-track and her equally fast-track husband, and others. They were mostly college graduates, several of them college scholarship athletes. They were smart and capable and athletic and good and kind people.

But they didn't care about baseball. They had no sense of the history of the game, they held no romantic attachments to it. They tried, I think, for my father's sake, to appreciate what he was showing them and what he wanted to talk about; but they just didn't get from those cardboard cards what Dad intended.

Dad was trapped and lost when these usual ploys failed and we were all more than a little embarrassed by the situation. Hurt, he commanded me to take him and Mom back to the assisted-living place and, dutiful always, I did that. We didn't talk much on the drive and as I helped them get to their room, wheeling Dad's wheelchair around the hallways and into the elevator and then to their apartment, where he insisted I help him take care of himself in the bathroom. Instead, I called for an aide and she came quickly. Sorry, dad.

I'd like to think that finally, in my mid-fifties and only after having seen the damage these hollow constructions caused, I have grown up enough to take life as it is and remember Dad as he was. That is, after all, at least partly what this book is about: the truth of a life and death in baseball; though I've discovered it's often painful to find the truth when you've had a hand in creating the myths and when, like me, you remain susceptible to the romantic notions of the game. But I don't know if I've grown up yet or not.

My daughter the soccer player now plays for her high-school team and one of our city's better all-star teams. Soccer and track and, to a lesser extent, basketball seem to interest her. We play catch from time to time, but she throws like a girl and isn't ashamed of that and for good reason: she can run like a cheetah and made the high-school varsity's 4×100 relay squad while still in eighth grade. She plays hard-nosed defense in soccer unless the coach needs her speed up front and moves her to forward. She crashes the boards in basketball, and just for fun she's a dandy downhill skier.

91

She's a bright girl, too; academically near the top of the two hundred or so students in her grade at her school. She's smart, she's athletic, and she's lucky. Both of her parents are college professors and so we have time, and just enough income, to do a lot of traveling, especially in the summers, weaving our trips around our daughter's soccer commitments. So she's been to London often enough to not have much interest in going again, and Edinburgh and Dublin and Madrid and several islands in the Caribbean and the mountains and cities of California and the heat of Houston and a lot of other places, as well. She's a good traveler and she likes to take pictures and meet people. She's lived an interesting life so far, and one with plenty of happy memories for a girl in her teens.

But her memories of my father, sadly, are mostly unhappy ones. He would summon up a smile when she came with me to see him, and she'd give him a hug in return for his smiles at the end of soccer practice or the games he came to watch during those last months of his life. But those few happier moments were outweighed by what she couldn't help but see me going through. She spent more than a year of her childhood watching me struggle to cope with my father's demands. She heard the phone ringing and saw my reaction to answering the eighth or tenth angry call of the day. She heard my half of the conversation as he demanded I come right over and deliver a cheeseburger, though I'd told him of my commitments to her and to my special son and to my wife and to, at some level, myself.

She sensed the competition. He was a child now, an alien child in elderly clothing, returning firmly to the childhood status he'd enjoyed in the Roaring Twenties and the Great Depression: the rum-running days of Baby. He didn't want to share me, he wanted to be my only child. He wanted to be the sole focus of my attention, like we'd always taught him for all those many years. Skip. Our manager. The ballplayer and storyteller.

She'd watched her other grandfather die a couple of years before. Robert Smith had fought in the Pacific Theater as flight engineer and top-turret gunner on a B-25. He'd been on wave-top bombing runs at Iwo Jima; he'd dropped a few loads of bombs on Japanese-held China; he'd been in the air on a mission one day in August of 1945 and he and his crewmates had seen a mushroom cloud rising from the Japanese coast as Hiroshima melted and died. He did not fear death when it came stalking him fifty years later, the prostate cancer finally overwhelming a good man, a blue-collar guy who'd raised six kids and who lived and died with enormous dignity. My daughter saw how her mother and her grandmother and her aunts and uncles struggled with Bob's death and she knew how that went: sadly but with honor.

And then she watched my father's final months and there wasn't much dignity about it. Dad suffered from the comparison when it came to how her two grandfathers handled their hardest of times. This bright and lovely and talented girl didn't understand the baseball myth and how it could possibly have excused or explained her grandpa Skip's behavior.

And then I took her along one hot summer day to see the film *The Rookie*, in which Dennis Quaid stars in the true story (or as true as Hollywood can make it) of Jim Morris, the high-school baseball coach who promised his players he'd give pro ball one more try if they would only try hard themselves to win some key games for their high-school team. They did and he did and then he earned his way to the major leagues through a combination of a good fastball, the needs of the Tampa Bay Devil Rays expansion franchise, and an understanding wife and son.

It's an archetypal baseball film in that it embraces wholly the mythic wonder of the game, which transcends family obligations: The film assumes that any normal American male — even one with a good job and a settled life — would leave his wife and child to fend for themselves while he tried to succeed in professional baseball. The acting is good, the setting often Costneresque (or, to be fair, Kinsellaesque) with its misty night-games played in minor-league stadiums leading ultimately to the Rays playing the Texas Rangers in Arlington, where Morris (in the film if not in real life) reaches his pinnacle and pitches in a big-league game. Most of the population from the small Texas town that he left to give baseball one more try is there, of course, to cheer him on in the Big Game. At the end everyone is properly proud of their local hero. At the end the music swells and the metaphors roll right through you: just believe in your dreams and they'll come true, as long you can throw a baseball at ninety-eight miles an hour with good accuracy.

My daughter was not a baseball fan during the times that the real Jim Morris was pitching for the real Devil Rays. I would take her and my son to Tropicana Field five or six times a summer and while he and I would watch the fumbling Rays with interest, she mostly sat with a book in her lap and read. We saw Morris pitch on two occasions and while he earned his cup of coffee in the big leagues, his fastball didn't impress a young girl.

Once, in early October of 1999, we were at a game against the Yankees when Rays outfielder Randy Winn came up with the bases loaded and hit

93

a shot into right center that bounced off the tricky angles of the Trop's walls to carom around while some delightfully hapless Yankees chased it down.

It was obvious to my son and I that a rare and wonderful event was in the making, a possible inside-the-park grand slam homerun, and we stood to cheer and scream while Winn rounded first, then second, then third and headed for home while Paul O'Neill of the Yanks finally got to the ball, turned to hit the relay man who then threw to home, bringing Jorge Posada up the line just far enough that Winn was able to slide safely past the tag.

It was quite a moment and my son and I stood to applaud and yell and slap joyous high fives with each other. But my daughter sat there, reading her Harry Potter and only slightly annoyed about the noise and the fuss that were getting in the way of Harry's quidditch game. By the time we could get her to look up from her book ("But this is crucial," she pleaded), the play was over, all four runs were in, and a tiny bit of real history was added to baseball's mythology.

Baseball, to her, didn't matter, even in its oddities.

Still, she was willing to go with me for a father/daughter outing, to the fancy Baywalk Theater in St. Petersburg. All I had to do was promise that we'd get chocolate shakes and burgers at Johnny Rockets afterward, which I thought a small price to pay for a little bonding. I wondered, as I bought the tickets, if the movie would hold her interest.

It did. *The Rookie* is Hollywood baseball at its romantic best, and as we left the theater my daughter and I were both affected by it. It was the first baseball film she'd ever seen in a theater and she dried her eyes as we left.

"So," she said, "Grandpa Skip played in the major leagues, right?"

"Right."

"So he was one of those kinds of players, right?"

"Right," I said. "When I was your age he had just finished up his career as a player and was a coach for the White Sox."

'Wow," she said. "Cool."

"Yeah," I said. "Yeah, it sure was."

11

Keeping Score

DEL WILBER KEPT SCORE, AND his wife sometimes seemed to be the team he was playing against, especially in the early months of his time in St. Petersburg. Within a few weeks of their arrival I realized that Mom needed at least as much medical attention as Dad. Her memory and cognition troubles, her emotional combativeness, her dismaying addiction to stimulants and the tics and jerks and contractions that seemed to come from that: all these and more meant arranging for and taking her to a long string of health visits: the neurologist, the family-practice man who became her primary physician, the psychologist, the physical therapist and more.

Dad kept a close eye on how many doctor appointments she had and, weirdly I thought, he wanted to make sure he had more. Since there were times over the course of those months when, between the two of them, I would be at as many as five or six appointments in a single week, the situation became pretty complex. I began putting up a printed list their room. One of those lists looked like this:

UPCOMING DOCTOR APPOINTMENTS
DEL WILBER

Friday, November 2 eye exam with Dr. Repke at 9 A.M. (Rick)
Friday, Nov 2 with urologist Dr. Kapadia at 11:30 A.M. (Rick)
Monday, November 5, cataract operation (w/Mary)
Tuesday, November 6, post-op (w/ Mary)
Tuesday, November 13, post-op (w/Fountains)

Monday, November 19, eyelid surgery (with Bob)
Tuesday, November 20, 9 A.M. post-op (Bob)
Tuesday, November 20, @ Springle 3 P.M./ checkup (Rick)
Monday, December 3, cataract operation (w/?)
Tuesday, December 4, cataract post-op (w/?)
Tuesday, December 11, post-op (Fountains)
Thursday, January 10, 2002, 3:45 P.M. @ Bell

TAFFY WILBER

Monday, November 12, 10:10 A.M. @ Springle (w/Rick)
Thursday, January 10, 2002, with Dr. Bell @ 3:30 P.M.

Often, Dad had more appointments. But once he was through with the multiple visits for his cataract surgery, his list narrowed until, at one point, he looked over a posted schedule and saw two appointments for his wife and none for him for one week (a welcome light week, from my perspective). I had just finished posting the list and he wheeled over to take a look at it. He frowned. "You know, I need to go see the doctor, too."

"You saw two different doctors last week, Dad," I said "and now you get a week off."

"Well, I don't need a week off. I need to see a doctor," he said, thinking, I could only suppose, that he was in some kind of odd medical batting slump where his health was too good.

It became ever more bizarre, this sense of keeping score, and he would not let go of it, so I became inventive in their scheduling, trying to make sure that Dad had at least one more visit than Mom. When that proved impossible I would bring him along on her appointments, which added another layer of difficulty in several respects but at least kept him in the game.

As time went on, Dad's scorekeeping expanded from doctor appointments to family issues. He seemed to want to make sure he saw more of me than my students did, or even than my own family did, and he was counting to make sure he was in the lead. So the stress level was high, with Dad making the usual demands while Mom slid away from us into that strange and private world where we couldn't reach her much anymore.

In addition to the doctor visits, I also found myself keeping track of and trying to construct a social life for Dad and Mom. They were in a very nice ALF, where an important part of the facility's offerings center on socializing. But Dad didn't seem interested in any of the offerings, whether live music or movies in the small theater or afternoon men's group meeting.

Mom, at least, enjoyed several different things for the first few months and brought her husband along as they made some friends and began eating dinner with them in the very nice dining room of their facility.

But family socialization was another thing entirely. After all, the major reasons we'd brought Dad and Mom south from St. Louis was to get them to a place where there was some family. Our immediate logic for this was for reasons of health and safety, but a secondary consideration, surely, was familial and I tried hard to pay attention to this, including Dad and Mom in as many things as we could.

My original plan was to help the old pro get acclimated to his new surroundings so he could become the genial old storyteller he'd been back home, regaling a circle of admirers with stories from baseball's golden age. I thought at first that I was in luck, since the men's group that met weekly liked to talk about sports and mostly, I was told, about baseball. Dad would be the center of attention there, I thought, and he'd love that.

But he wasn't interested, for reasons I still can't fathom some four years later, though surely they revolved around his sense of pride. So the socialization for Dad that I'd hoped for didn't work out, and instead his social life came to center on me, which was unfortunate in any number of ways but mostly in that I didn't have the time available that he demanded of me.

These demands had caught me by surprise. After all, in the better retirement years before Dad's health had really caught up with him, he and Mom had been coming to St. Pete Beach, where I lived, for a few weeks of vacation each winter when St. Louis had turned gray and cold. My older brother would get them tickets, I'd meet them at the airport, and they'd stay at a nice hotel on the beach or at a small inn across the street from the beach. They happily kept themselves busy at either place and I wouldn't see them more than two or three times a week during their vacation. Dad especially liked the little inn, where he enjoyed talking to the owner's parrot, walking on the beach, sitting by the small pool and hot tub and having breakfast, most mornings, at the Seahorse Restaurant, just across the street from Merry Pier and with an outdoor deck that gave wonderful views of Boca Ciega Bay and the dolphins rolling by in the calm water. A couple of runny eggs, a lot of bacon, some sausage, some hash browns, a cup of coffee, toast: Dad loved it there, so much so that when they came to the ALF on a permanent basis, I planned to make it a regular Friday morning feature of their lives, picking them up about 8 A.M. and taking them to the Seahorse for breakfast.

We did that for the first three weeks, but then Dad liked those Friday mornings so much that he began to demand I take them there a lot more often, preferably every morning. When I explained that I had a job teaching and that my university and my students expected me to show up for those morning classes he grumbled mightily, letting me know that I didn't understand. He was Del Wilber. He'd played baseball in Philly and Boston and St. Louis. He was here now. He wanted to eat breakfast at the Seahorse on a regular basis. Game over.

Author and father, at the Seahorse Restaurant in Pass-a-Grille, Florida.

Our disagreement over how often I should take him out to breakfast was among the first of our many struggles that year. I thought we'd brought him and Mom to Florida for safety and comfort. He thought he'd come to Florida to enjoy himself, to enjoy this bonus time having defeated the prostate cancer that had nearly killed him (and would finally claim him a year later). Problem was, with Mom slipping into dementia I became the sole source for that expected enjoyment. I thought it would be like their previous visits, only on an extended basis. I figured on spending a few hours with them each week, getting them to breakfast on Fridays and stopping by once or twice a week otherwise to help out, to listen to stories, to take them to the occasional doctor visits.

Dad, on the other hand, figured that I would spend

whatever time it took to keep him happy. So we collided, often, and never did get it straight.

Ultimately our struggles spread, leading to friction between me and my siblings. Some of those problems still exist today. Dad's death didn't case them; if anything, in fact, his death and my reaction to it re-opened old wounds while creating new ones. That sort of conflict, I've come to think, is just a part of the caregiving package.

These sorts of sibling troubles are common, I've discovered. In a *Time* magazine article called "Who Cares More for Mom?" I read this: "If you're a 50-year-old with 80-year-old parents, you may think that the sibling rivalries and parental hurts of your childhood are history. Fat chance. Simmering resentment between siblings has a nasty way of re-erupting as boomers confront the reality of caring for aging parents."*

Well, yes, I think. That's very much what happened. Old resentments from decades ago re-emerged in our family and my caregiving was the cause. When I tried at one point, more than a year after Dad's death, to bridge the divide I received an e-mail from one sibling detailing some things I'd said as much as twenty-five years before. I'd said those things and they were wrong and I apologized. It didn't matter, and we still don't talk, that sibling and I. Sadly, some of my other siblings have chosen up sides on this. In terms of family harmony, it's downright tragic. Too bad.

Francine Russo, "Who Cares More for Mom?" Time, June 12, 2005. http://www.time.com/ time/magazine/article/0,9171,1071271,00.html

12

Fins to the Left

My sister Cindy and I are staring out the window of my parent's eleventh-floor apartment in the assisted-living facility. Cindy's flown in from California just to spend time with Dad and Mom and she's impressed with the ALF. The rooms on this floor of this wing of the complex are for those residents who are mentally capable but need some physical assistance. Our parents have been here for a couple of months now and I'm happy to say the physical-needs part of that plan has worked out pretty well: Dad has aides to help him with everything from using the toilet to getting into bed. They rub balm on his legs for him, they work with him in physical therapy to stand and then walk for a few steps, they help him dress and undress. He doesn't mind the help.

The mentally capable part of the equation has us worried. Dad seems fine but Mom's behavior and her thinking, especially her short-term memory, concern us. We're thinking we're going to need a doctor take a look at her sometime soon. For now, we looking out toward Boca Ciega Bay below us and there, in the distance, the shimmer of the Gulf of Mexico. It's quite a view.

I notice a shape in the shallow water of the bay below us. A large shape; a very large shape. I'm used to seeing manatees cruising along in these waters but this is different, sleeker, and as I watch I realize that shape is a large bull shark, the thicker middle part of the body giving it away. It's the only large shark I've seen in the bay in the twenty years I've lived in the area.

Though it's hard to tell from where I'm standing, I'd guess it's seven or eight feet long, maybe more.

I point it out to my sister and her eyes grow wide. "Wow," she says. She's a nature girl and knows her stuff. She left the Midwest for California in 1971, heading west to San Francisco. She's done well out there, raised some great kids, worked hard, written a couple of good books. She's prospered, in fact, and now has what my daughter thinks is the job from heaven: working in Education Coordination for Stanford University's Jasper Ridge Nature Preserve. My daughter is a nature girl, too, and she hugely admires her Aunt Cindy. That's OK, I admire Cindy, too.

From up here the shark looks almost too big to fit in the shallow estuary. At times parts of its body rise up out of the water even while it swims leisurely around. Just twenty or thirty yards away from it, a fisherman has waded into the water as so many of us like to do here, knee-deep or waist-deep in the warm water, trying to catch something good to eat or something that will put up a good fight. He's casting to spots very near the shark and that would make for a very good fight, indeed. From where we stand it looks like a tragedy in the making.

Mom is in her bedroom, lying on her bed, reading, and we don't disturb her, but Dad is in this living area, sitting on the couch, his walker right next to him and the wheelchair next to that. We call him over to see, we head that way to help him get up to see this; but he just grumbles that he's not interested. Later I'll understand why. So Cindy and I watch alone, transfixed, as the shark circles and meanders, getting a bit closer to the fisherman each time. Our window is sealed shut so we can't warn the guy from here. Should we try to use the too-busy elevator to get down and warn him? Should we run down the eleven flights of stairs and out the one hundred yards or so to the dock and try from there to yell a warning. No, it looks too late for that; it's all going to happen in the next few moments.

The shark comes closer. The guy is reeling in his line, and it's coming in from right where the shark swims. We're glued to the window; seconds now as the shark comes closer and then, at last, sensing something it doesn't like, the big bull turns away and with a flick of its tail picks up speed and heads toward the center of the bay. The fisherman never notices, which amazes me at that moment. Months from now I'll understand better how easy it is for someone to wade into trouble and to not see disaster looming; but right now the whole metaphor escapes me and I'm just glad to see that the fisherman is alive, the shark is gone and the bay is serene.

Mom walks in from her bedroom. She's angry. She wants to talk about the missing checkbook and where the hell is her car and she's having a nice time and everything but when are they going to head home to St. Louis?

Cindy and I ask her if she'd like to go downstairs and listen to the guy in the lobby play "Sentimental Journey" on the piano and Mom calms down. She thinks that's a good idea, in fact, and so we go. To renew old memories.

Caregiving is about a lot of complex things: role reversals, patience, anger, love, hard realities and soft mythologies. It is also about bookkeeping, since one of the first and most necessary tasks a typical caregiver takes on is keeping track of things for elderly parents who can no longer handle life's various organizational issues on their own. Typically, this starts with money matters and goes on from there to doctor appointments, social occasions, shopping and more: the taxi and scheduling duties fitting right in with the parent/child role reversal that the experts warn of, with all its tricky emotional risks.

I have plenty of trouble handling my own checkbook, and so to my great relief my other sister, Mary, and my wife Robin took on these tasks for Mom and Dad. As is often the case with elderly parents, Mom resented having the checkbook taken away, though she was very clearly no longer able to handle the bill-paying duties she'd been in charge of since 1945. Some bills weren't being paid at all, others were being paid twice or even more often. You could see the deterioration of her mental abilities right there in the way she wrote out the checks, the scribbled names and amounts becoming increasingly indecipherable as the weeks went by: clarity becoming chaos right there on the page. One of the very few times I was reduced to tears over my parents' decline was the first time I saw that checkbook and realized what I was seeing: a mind in the process of being overwhelmed by its enemy.

We simply had to take over and so we did; but there was friction, a lot of friction. Mom didn't think any of this was necessary and she resented our efforts, though we invented a variety of excuses to make the loss of control as palatable as possible. We talked about how she wouldn't have to worry about all this bill-paying stuff now and she could enjoy her time in Florida without worrying about her money. We talked about how no one used checks anymore and she had her credit card (a JCPenney card; we took the rest away). We told her we'd arranged for her to go to the bank that had a branch right in her building whenever she wanted some cash. All she had to do was sign her name and the friendly woman at the bank's window would give her the cash she wanted. We tried all of these and more, but as the months went by the stress of that first, simple step kept returning as Mom periodically remembered that she no longer had the control that she'd held for so long. Over the half-century or more of her personal history, Mom had always been in charge of her life, and often of ours, and always of certain parts of her husband's. Now we were saying that was over. It wasn't easy for anyone.

Reading over the e-mails that I sent to my brothers and sisters from those times reminds me of how stressful that time period was, and how temporary the occasional successes were. Long after we thought the battle was over and we had taken control of Mom and Dad's finances, the arguments and anger would re-emerge. Mom would rediscover that she couldn't find her checks or most of her credit cards and would, in anger or confusion or both (depending on what she could recall), call us to complain. And, of course, the troubles were just part of the larger picture of her dementia that we were coming to realize; part of those troubles stemming from her odd addiction to nicotine gum, part from long-standing thyroid problems, most, we came to understand at last, from her long, slow slide into Alzheimer's.

To get to that sad diagnosis the neurologist I took her to, Dr. Dan Bell, had scheduled a series of tests that slowly ruled out various other causes for Mom's memory troubles and began to center on Alzheimer's. But Mom had other problems, too; including sudden, unpredictable, jerks and twitches in her right arm and leg. I'd first noticed these at a Wendy's restaurant that she and I went to on the way to the nursing home back in St. Louis, where Dad had been dying (we thought at the time) from prostate cancer. We stopped to get Dad his favorite meal, a Wendy's bacon cheeseburger and a diet cola, and after we'd stood in line, gotten the sack of food and the empty cups to fill over at the soda machine, she had one of the spasms: a couple of cups full of soft drink went flying and she stumbled briefly.

Mary, the daughter who'd done so much for Mom and Dad for more than a decade, had noticed this months before and taken Mom to the family doctor, who'd sent Mom to an orthopedist who'd diagnosed a torn rotator cuff. That diagnosis was deliciously ironic given Dad's life in baseball; but later we found that the tear was the effect, not the cause. The spasms became severe enough over time that by the time we'd moved her to St. Petersburg she was routinely dropping cups of coffee as she walked across the room (the caffeine in the coffee didn't help the stimulant overdose, of course) and then they escalated further, to the point where they caused her to fall several times a day. Bell and other doctors began to suspect her other problems were the result of her heavy use of nicotine gum. In the late 1980s Mom had kicked her lifelong cigarette habit by switching to the gum, at the time a prescription drug. Later the gum went over the counter and Mom continued to buy and chew it often, though it's meant to be part of a short-term solution to nicotine addiction.

A couple of weeks after I'd taken over as caregiver I was shopping with Mom in a local Walgreen's and I noticed her buying thirty dollars' worth of Nicorette. We started talking about it and I came to realize that she was spending money—a lot of money—on the gum. In her case (and, perhaps, in the case of many more elderly ex-smokers), the addiction to the gum had replaced the addiction to the cigarettes and her heavy usage was causing her damage. Nicotine is a stimulant, and Mom was ingesting eighty or one hundred or more milligrams of nicotine into her system every day, causing neurological damage. The gum, I discovered, is expensive, too, at about $1 a piece. So her habit was not only life threatening, it was costing her and Dad somewhere around two hundred dollars a week, and she was rapidly using up their savings. With the help of the staff at the assisted-living facility and with the guidance of Tom Marcic, a psychologist who specializes in care for the elderly and worked with the ALF, we spent six months trying, and failing, to get her off the gum. Ultimately, her primary-care physician, the neurologist, Marcic, and the nursing staff all agreed that we had to do something more definitive and that we needed Dad's help to make that happen by putting Mom into a detox ward. The complexities of the relationship between Mom, her nicotine gum, Dad, and myself and my sister became a source of considerable stress and aggravation there for a time.

At one point, after seeing the depths of her problem and worrying over how it was causing motor control problems for her and might even be threatening her heart, Marcic proposed a Plan A, which was to convince her to ease off the gum and then eventually get her to quit it entirely. But he knew there wasn't much hope of that actually working and he had, from the start, a tougher Plan B in mind, too: Detox, in a closed unit of the same assisted-living facility where she was already staying. Behind locked doors the nurses, doctors and aides could control her addiction and slowly wean her off the nicotine and other stimulants and, it was hoped, save her life.

It was my job as caregiver to take part in Plan A, which meant talking to her often about the gum and the problems it was causing her and working with her, nicely but firmly as I was instructed, to cut back on it. I had very little success, as this e-mail from December of that year shows:

To: Update list
From: Rick Wilber
Subject: update on Taffy
Date: Dec 2001

Taffy and I just had an official Huge Argument over the nicotine gum. She took it from my hands, got very angry with me, said she had to have it and it didn't hurt her and the doctors were wrong and that I should just stop trying to get her to stop.

It was one of the more uncomfortable moments of my life, frankly.

This came after Rich and I took her grocery shopping (an interesting excursion, I might add, with repeated efforts to buy bread despite my pointing out that we already had done so). She was chewing that gum the whole time, of course. She always chews it, at 2–4 mg of nicotine a piece.

We came back. Earlier, I'd posted on the bulletin board each of your phone numbers (she just can't remember Mary's for some awful reason—called me twice last night for it, and again this afternoon) and also a notice that said Dr. Bell and Dr. Springle say no nicotine gum, and only decaf coffee and sodas. She just shook her head and smiled.

Then I went into her drawer, took out the six packs of a dozen pieces each and walked into the living room and we had it out. Eventually, I handed them back to her. I'm sorry. I admit defeat. Turns out it's very, very hard to see your mother like that and—not—hand her the damn gum.

I told her, as I did so, that I would e-mail you all and that you would call her about this. PLEASE CALL HER.

And now I'm stymied. I'll call the Fountains tomorrow and tell them the current plan has failed. But I don't know what to do about it.

We can: 1) let her chew her brain into oblivion, god knows nicotine has killed millions in one fashion or another and she wouldn't be the first or last. The downside is we'll all have to deal with the horror of it for perhaps years to come. 2) put her into detox, but I now think she'd get through it, come out and buy more damn gum. 3) maybe get her to a shrink? 4) I have no idea....

I'm open to any thoughts.

Oh, at the end of it, Skip asked me to come into his room. He said I shouldn't beat myself up too much over this, and then said thanks.

For a time we kept trying, but Mom refused to cut back or to even consider the health implications. She would point out often that it was doctors who had prescribed the gum in the first place. I would counter with the information on how little she'd been prescribed to chew each day, and how that was supposed to end more than ten years ago, and that she was abusing a stimulant and it could kill her. She was unpersuaded and unpersuadable.

We punched and counter-punched on the gum, poor Mom's terrible combination of stimulant-induced frenzy and increasing dementia leading her into other, darker, actions, including violence toward her husband of more than fifty years and to anger and belligerence toward my sister and toward me. Her loss of control over her own finances was the symbolic façade for these troubles. This e-mail shows how hard we found it to make much progress.

To: Siblings
From: Rick
Date: Tue, 15 Jan 2002

Taffy's belligerence grows daily lately, mainly centered around the checks right now. She doesn't seem bothered at all that I took the computer out of there a few days ago. She's not belligerent toward me but toward Mary, since Mary has the checks. I suspect the desire for checks and the desire for gum are intertwined, even though Taffy is able to get cash any time from the bank in the lobby — and can use a blank bank check there to do it. I reminded Skip of that. He'd forgotten.

She hasn't told him about her seeing Marcic, but that's OK, seems to me. I've told Skip about her sessions, of course, and warned him again of the possible consequences, including detox. I didn't mention to Marcic the possibility of violence, since I didn't want to trigger any mandated response.

When I talked to Skip this evening he was home alone (Taffy downstairs listening to music — good for her).... He also said he wasn't worried about getting stuff thrown at him (Taffy tosses stuff like bottles of Gatorade his way, and he's not quite the catcher he once was) and that she's not hitting him all that often with books. I told him to call me immediately if that happens and he said he would. He's frail enough that it wouldn't take much, and that has to worry us all, I'd think. A little irrational anger and bad things could happen.

—Rick

A few weeks later the downward spiral continued, but no one wanted to put Mom through the detox unless we absolutely had to. My contact with Marcic was frequent as we struggled to help her, but her path seemed obvious to me. There were several times when one of my sisters or I would receive incoherent, angry phone calls from Mom. Those calls were a map to where she would have to travel before we could get her off the stimulants, as this e-mail shows:

Friday, January 25, 2002 8:00 P.M.
To: Update List
Subject: tough love

Hi, all. Had a long telephone chat with the psychologist, Dr. Marcic today. He thinks Taffy's invented memories are most likely her going into Stage Two with her Alzheimer's. But he thinks, too, that it might be the gum. And so he plans the following steps: 1) He'll try the rationing approach one more time, where the Fountains staff gives her an amount each day and tapers it off until she's off it. 2) When that doesn't work, he'll add a complete money cut-off to that, so she doesn't have access to any money to spend to buy any gum on her own (that'll be a joy to go through, btw). 3) When that doesn't work, he'll put her into the Alzheimer's section downstairs at the Fountains for a week or two to detox her and control the amount. In that section of the Fountains, you can't leave on your own.
Tough love, guys, tough love.

A complicating factor: no, *the* complicating factor in all this was Dad's behavior. On the one hand he seemed to want very much to do what he could for his wife. On the other hand, he was as disappointed and unhappy as he could possibly be about how this all had an impact on his life. He seemed to think that we'd lost our focus, which should have been on him. He was the one who'd nearly died six months before from prostate cancer and had rallied. He was the one engaged in the on-going struggle with that cancer, with Parkinson's, with cataracts and all the rest. He was the old pro. He was the one who'd hit three home runs in one game for the Phillies in 1951. He was Dad. He wanted attention from all his children and he absolutely demanded attention from me, and that combined with Mom's pressing needs to make my life pretty damn difficult at times. On a good day he understood the necessity of our efforts to help Mom and he dealt with it reasonably well. But not every day was a good day, as I noted in an e-mail. Sometimes his need for attention drove him to behaviors that I found frustrating. I recognized these behaviors for what they were, I think; but I couldn't seem to figure out ways to change them.

From: Rick Wilber
Sent: Tuesday, January 29, 2002 6:58 P.M.
To: Update List
Subject: update #12

Hello, all.
After my morning classes, I checked the machine and there were four hang-ups. Well, I know that—has—to be Skip, so, pissed off that he summons

me with these hang-up calls (just leave a message, damnit), I called, because it just might be something important and I'm from the Midwest and a Catholic and consumed with guilt and just have to call.

Taffy answers. She sounds bad. I ask to speak to Skip, thinking maybe it's violence he wants to talk about. Instead, he says he can't get to the phone now and I should call later.

I check the machine at home later and there's a call from the Fountains. Taffy has a new prescription waiting at Walgreen's and would I please get it asap....

OK, I drive home and call Skip and Taffy first. She sounds horrible. He finally talks, and plays that damn obtuse backward conversational game where I'm supposed to beg him to allow me to help him. "You know, your mother was really sick last night," he says.

"Oh?" I ask, "what happened?"

"Well, she was up at three in the morning throwing up. Later on we had a whole convention in here with nurses and all of them."

"So what happened?"

"Well, she was sick."

"And.... How is she now?"

"Well, not great. You know, she was pretty sick."

And then it dawns on me what I'm supposed to say: "Do you want me to call the doctor for you?"

"Well, that's what I was thinking," he says, relieved at last that I've caught onto this and figured out what to ask him. Gads.

OK, so I start a round of phone calls. Turns out the Fountains has it under control and after I confirm this with the doc's office a few phone calls and on-hold sessions later, Robin stops by Walgreens, gets the prescription for Taffy and drops it off on her way home. The medicine is Promethazine, which for $46 prevents nausea and vomiting. Let's hope it works for her.

This is the second time in a few weeks for this with her. Is it related to the nicotine gum? An overdose? Withdrawal? Underdose? Beats me.

I wonder, too, how in Hell did Skip ever communicate with his players? Did he make them ask him please coach me? It's a — very — frustrating way to have a conversation, and that he plays these games when his wife is puking and sick is really, really frustrating. I got so mad about it that I called him back and let him have it (nicely enough, though). Don't hang up if it's important. Don't strain my limited psychic skills. Leave a message so I know what you want. He said he would. I realized this plays right into his hands, of course, since now when he calls I absolutely guarantee he will leave a message saying it's important and I need to call right back and it will be for diapers. Bet you a zillion dollars that happens within a day or two.

On the plus side, Rich walked over and visited with them today. Skip said it was fun, with Rich taking Skip in the wheelchair out to the dock to look at the water. That's my boy.

Mary and I plan to meet with the psychologist on Friday to talk over what to do about Taffy's situation.

We knew we had to move from Plan A to Plan B after a few of these health crises for Mom. But the detox move was no simple thing. The logistics began with a doctor's order, which was the easy part. Then it required an available room in the locked-down area of the building. Then, most importantly, it required permission from Dad. At one crucial juncture, my sister Mary and I thought we had it done. We got Dad's signed permission, we had the room ready, we had the doctor's faxed instructions. We were ready. I sent a note to my siblings.

February 01, 2002 1:17 P.M.
To: Update List
Subject: into detox

Hello, all.
Today's the day.
Mary and I met with Dr. Tom Marcic and he says it's a matter of life and death for Taffy, that she—must—go into detox, and so he is at the Fountains now arranging for her to put into a room on a locked floor for a month's detox.

We'll work out the details as we go. Skip will be relieved, I suspect, since the pressure on him has been tough. We'll move enough clothes down to the new room for her and handle all the other details, and let you know what's up as it happens. If there's no room available right now, we'll wait until there is one and take action then.

Marcic has been doing research on nicotine gum and its long-term effects. He says he's not only worried about the effect on her brain and mind, but also on her heart after all these years of stimulants. He plans to take the heat for it from Taffy so she doesn't blame (at least immediately) me or Mary, though we can see clearly the very tough times ahead.

Stay tuned.

But then in a worrisome, stressful afternoon and evening filled with ironies, we didn't manage to get Mom into detox after all. We met with Marcic who said he felt it was life or death now for her and so she had to be moved. It wouldn't be easy and it wouldn't come cheap at about $3000 a month. But it would, we hoped, get her off the gum.

We headed to Mom and Dad's room to get her. And she wasn't there. This, from an e-mail I wrote after the fact, explains that day:

February 01, 2002 10:15 P.M.
To: Update List
Subject: into detox

Skip is there, but no Taffy. We break the news to Skip, who has his doubts. Turns out over the next hour that most of those doubts are centered around himself—who'll take care of him? The Fountains will, of course. He calms down. He says she's at Kash & Karry, buying gum and groceries. We wait. We wait some more. We wait a -lot- more. The doc leaves, but we have his pager number. We wait more. It's been an hour. Two hours. No Taffy. Now we're worried.

We go downstairs to meet the doc. We call (the local) taxi company and find out that she went to Dillard's in the big mall to buy make-up. The taxi left her there and the driver is home, shift over.

Shit.

Can she get home on her own? It's been 2½ hours or more now. Is she lost there? We don't know, so we drive to the mall, go to Dillards, and the girl at the Estee Lauder counter says sure, she remembers her and sold her some make-up an hour and a half before. Ooh, boy.

We go to the security folks. They page her, no response. They get all the security folks looking for her. No luck.

Finally, we get a call from Robin. Taffy made her way back to the Fountains safely, just a few hours later than expected. I'll get the details of Taffy's Big Adventure some other time.

By now it's too late to do the Big Detox Move. So that's for tomorrow. Mary has a major stress headache. I'm drinking Corona. And that's that for now.

This failed effort to get the move accomplished caused all sorts of complications, giving Dad more doubts about the move while it extended poor Mom's confusion and anger. The next day I wrote this to my siblings:

February 2, 2002 9:36 P.M.
To: Update List
Subject: into detox

You all need to know that Taffy has called me several times (so far) tonight, extremely angry about not having any checks. The latest call came a few minutes ago at 9:30, with Skip doing the dialing and then getting her on the phone, to calm her down I suspect. She wants to go shopping tomorrow with her friend Vera and she suddenly realized she doesn't have any checks (as she hasn't for several months now). I reminded her of the day when she and I agreed that I'd take them and we'd take over the bills—that day is long forgotten, of course. I told her about bills going unpaid and other bills getting paid twice. She said it was all news to her and it was damn time that somebody told her these things, because she'd been wondering where all the bills were.

I told her to get some cash from the bank, take her credit card, and go have fun. She said no, many places want checks (?). She went on at length—very, very angry and hostile—about how she'd raised five kids, she'd earned the money, she had a right to those checks etc etc etc. She said she had half a mind to just take her credit card and go home tomorrow (to St. Louis, I think she meant).

Jesus.

Been a very long day with the two of them, about which more later. But maybe tonight's craziness will convince Skip that his comfort is less important than her mental, emotional and physical health. Basically he made clear to me that his primary concern with having her down on the fourth floor is that she won't be there to take care of him.

I hope she doesn't get physical with him in the midst of her anger.

If you get this shortly, maybe give her a call and see if she's calmed down....

Finally, a few days later we had it all organized yet again and were ready for the move. But again things fell apart. As I summarized in an e-mail:

February 05, 2002 8:42 P.M.
To: Update List
Subject: into detox

All right, to summarize: Monday's are very, very busy for me, with a lecture class in front of 360, a lab with 20 more, then picking up Sam after Girl Scouts (Robin teaches a night class), helping Sam do homework in the van while scarfing a bite to eat, then soccer practice, then home by about 8:15 P.M., on a good day.

This meant I couldn't be there today for the Big Move. But that was OK, Dr. Marcic (the psychologist) told me, he and Rehana would handle it.

It has to be done soon, he reiterated, because it's now life or death. Mary tells me Dr. Pat concurred with Drs. Springle (primary), Bell (neurologist) and Marcic (shrink) that the recent bouts of vomiting for Taffy are clear indicators of overdosing and that her heart may give out (as well as the crap stealing her mind).

As I told you all before, on Saturday I talked on the phone with Skip following Friday's failure and he wished there was some other way. Well, yeah, don't we all. Mary and I and Marcic made it very clear to Skip on Friday that it was life or death for Taffy. I reiterated that on Saturday.

Skip, though, asked on Friday about who'd take care of him? We said the Fountains would.

So today, after a sleepless night last night and a helluva time trying to teach today with all this swirling around, at 3 P.M. or so I call Marcic's beeper. He calls me right back. Rehana tells him that Skip vetoed the move.

I want to say this very clearly: If this is true—that he said no because of his worries about being taken care of—then what he did was an act of selfish cowardice, risking her life for his comfort. My god, I've thought for the past hours, the man has no limits.

In short, I heard the news with the same dismay you all must have felt. After all this, to be stopped by that ... well....

... still, there was nothing doable at the moment.

When I got home this evening there was a message from Skip from 3:51 P.M. to this effect: "OK, Rehana never showed. I stopped by the office and she wants some information. I'll contact her tomorrow. Give me a call when you get back from your dinner (???) Right now Taffy's sleeping."

Then there was a hang-up at around 6 P.M., then nothing more.

What does this mean? I don't know. Perhaps—I hope—it isn't so simple as Skip just saying no. Or perhaps it is. We'll know tomorrow.

It was horrible. I was angry and disappointed in my father. The more I checked into what had happened the more I realized that he had, in fact, been worried enough about his own care to cancel the effort to take care of his wife. I found it extraordinarily selfish, even for Dad. But my anger abated as I dealt with the two of them over the next few days and as I listened to good advice from one sister or the other. They knew, they sympathized, and they had ideas for me that often helped, including the certain knowledge that anger wouldn't get me anywhere and we still had to get Mom into detox and get that process started. Calming down, thinking it through, I sent this note to one of my sisters.

February 06, 2002 12:09 P.M.
To: Update List
Subject: It's all in how you see it...

Well, what a night. At 10 or so, I think, I got the final hateful phone call from Taffy, blasting me for all my evils having to do with the checkbook, and then an angry hang-up. At 11:30 I decided it was done and went to bed, if not sleep.

This morning, Taffy told Mary that she remembered being mad at me but couldn't remember why. I think, at least, that helped Skip get the message about why this must be done. But I have to add that (as Mary noted in an e-mail to me this morning) Taffy's anger will know no bounds. She will be angry and furious and there will be at least one day of pure hell, directed at me and at Mary. I'll expect you all to be calling her and helping her (and us) to get through it.

I don't know when that day will be. I have to talk with Skip today (just called, no answer), and with the psychologist, and with Rehana. It goes on and on. The anger last night was absolutely blistering. She's done that with Mary before, I think, but this was the first out-and-out hate call I've received.

112

Meanwhile, yes, I'll do my best to be sympathetic with Skip and his behavior toward me. Cindy helped me see the usefulness of seeing him as a spoiled child rather than as an imperious and demanding and selfish old man. Fair enough, that arm raise is, indeed, something a 6-year-old would do, and so not necessarily at all the actions of Lord Wilber. I can see the truth in that, and a spoiled and frightened 6 year old might willingly sacrifice Taffy's health (or even her life) for his own comfort and sense of control. Makes sense to me, and does make it easier to take.

I'll let you all know how it goes, of course. As Mary just said to me, Onward.

And then, almost suddenly, the stars aligned somehow and we did get Mom into the detox unit, and with Dad's complete permission. Enough cajoling and begging and enough hard realities to see about her condition had finally convinced him that it had to be done.

The move was painful, in that Mom saw no reason for it to happen. Marcic was in charge and tried to emphasize the danger to her heart if she continued taking that much nicotine every day. He talked to her all the way down to the special locked unit and in she went. Our hope was that she'd blame him and not us, but we knew from the start that she would, like most addicts, find us to blame for her troubles.

And she did. The first night she was angry and hurt and disappointed in us all, and she let us know. By the next morning, things had improved a bit and she began calling Dad. He reported to me in a series of phone calls that she seemed better and I warned him that it would be a rough few weeks; the doctor had warned us she'd be angry and demanding and pleading and a sweetheart in turn. He said he understood, but added that he was concerned about his laundry. I promised we'd get it done for him. The assisted-living facility, of course, did it for him later that day.

Over the next few weeks my sister Mary and I put up with a long, sad series of scathing phone calls that slowly, over time, ebbed as Mom fought her way past the addiction and into a newer, cleaner self. Often, I unplugged the telephone because, as I said in one e-mail to my siblings, I was capable of taking on only so much vitriol from my mother before my blood pressure, my alarming stomach knots, and my general emotional health hit the wall and smashed to bits.

Eventually, the need for me to hide from my mother faded away and I plugged the phone back in as she returned to us, if not as the Mom we'd had for our whole lives at least as a much less angry and hostile version of this new Mom. And she was, for sure, a far healthier one physically. As the doctors had predicted, when she fought her way clear of the nicotine gum the twitches and spasms left along with the addiction.

Early on, desperate and worn down by it all, I had sent a depressing note to my siblings that said this: "I'm hoping she'll come down off the anger ... and now there's only 30 days to go. If I could quit this job, I would. Let's see: I try to extend and enrich their lives and, in Taffy's case, save her from herself—and I get this kind of crap in return. It's a deal, for sure."

But when she came out of the detox and smiled at me, I realized it was a pretty good deal, after all. I'd taken some heat and anger from her and poor lonely, needy Dad; but by March, Mom was back and the two of them were together again for whatever time was left and, for a while there, all the darkness that suffuses the caregiving role seemed worthwhile. As we rolled into March I decided to try and do something special for them both, something baseball, something Spring Training.

13

The Final Game: March 2002

I SAT ON A METAL FOLDING CHAIR just behind the box seats and a bit toward the third-base side of the plate at Al Lang Field in St. Petersburg, Florida. The seat was hard and hot but the view terrific, up close and in touch with the proceedings as we watched the hometown Devil Rays get ready for a spring-training game against the Toronto Blue Jays.

To my left, Dad sat in his wheelchair, quietly watching Rays pitcher Tanyon Sturtze take his last few warm-ups. Sturtze had never been a star, but he'd hung in there over the years, carving out a career the hard way, playing for the Cubs, the Rangers, the White Sox and now the Rays, convincing the powers-that-be each spring that he could still pitch, that he could get enough guys out to warrant being on the pitching staff, even if for a team as prone to loss as the Devil Rays.

More than fifty years ago, Dad's big-league career was like that. He was a journeyman catcher, moving from team to team, having to prove himself over and over again, spring after spring. Some players, the stars and even the established regulars, can show up for spring training thinking of it as an enjoyable, mostly stress-free, time to work their way into shape as they get ready for the long season to come. Others, guys like my dad, show up knowing they have to make the team.

To Dad's left sat my mother, his wife of fifty-nine years. Fresh out of detox for that weird addiction to nicotine gum, she looked busy—too busy—eyes wide and mouth open as she craned her neck to take it all in, commenting on the ballpark, the day, the teams, the fans; chatting with no one in particular, rambling on to anyone or no one about, mostly, the old days. Her short-term memory was about gone now. Tell her something, even pointedly ask her to remember it—and in five or ten minutes it had disappeared no matter how hard she tried.

But she was enjoying herself, sitting there in the sun and reminiscing about the more distant past, the one she could still recall, those good, postwar days of baseball in the sunshine with the other wives—Lil Musial and Mary Devine and Mary Marion and the others.

I watched her. I knew that by the time we got her home after the game she'd have forgotten the entire day—the game, the beautiful weather, the visits from family and friends. For the moment, though, in this Here and Now with all of us caught up in the day along with her, it was good to see her smile.

Dad coughed; a loose, phlegmy rattle that I'd heard too often in the past months. I knew, sitting there, that we were at Del Wilber's last spring training game. His first trip to St. Pete was in the 1940s as a prospect for the Cardinals. Sixty-one years later, his artificial hip, the onset of Parkinson's, his continuing hard struggle with prostate cancer and its deadly spread—these things had worn him down and the once tough catcher was weak and frail.

These physical battles and his wife's sad slide had burdened him emotionally and mentally, too. He'd become the angry, demanding, frustrated old man I'd battled with even as I tried to find sympathy for him. Most days, it seemed to me, he spent his time being unhappy; frowning and griping and making demands, most of them petty, and all of them aimed at me, the child of his five who'd wound up his caregiver in this last, hard year. He was not going gentle into that good night.

As the handy object of much of Dad's frustration and anger, I'd found the role exhausting and depressing. I'd tired of his attitude until by now I realized that I held anger toward him at least in equal measure to love. He'd worn away my admiration for him, chipping at it daily until, finally, it was gone. I wondered, often enough, when my debt for a happy childhood would be fully paid. It was a tough task, taking care of Dad and Mom in this steep decline, and I was no longer certain that I was up to it. There were days—a lot of them—when I just wanted to quit.

But I couldn't quit, of course, it wasn't that kind of job. And there were days like this, too, here and there: golden moments imbedded in the general unhappiness, where things seemed better again. As we sat in the sun of a mid–March afternoon in St. Petersburg and recalled better, happier days, I looked over and once, then twice, caught my father smiling.

As the game began I stood and helped Dad take off his red St. Louis Cardinals jacket. He loved wearing it, but Al Lang Field bakes in the sunshine and he was starting to sweat. Then I rubbed sunblock over his bare arms and stuck a brand-new Tampa Bay Devil Rays cap on his nearly bald head. The cap, one I'd bought at the concession stand, was something of a hit with him. Ten bucks well spent.

Sturtze had a good first inning, giving up a single but no runs. In the bottom of the inning Dad was watching as there was an out, a second out, a walk, and then the Rays' Ben Grieve stepped to the plate. After coming to the Rays in a trade the year before, Grieve had struggled at the plate. But he was young and a promising hitter and comes from a baseball family, so Dad said right away, "I like this kid. Good head on his shoulders."

After all those years of scouting, Dad's opinion carried a certain weight. When it came to watching a young major-leaguer's swing, Del Wilber knew what to look for. Heck, I was happy he was able to look at all. The cataract surgery from a few months before had been a qualified success, at least, and he could see a lot of the game and enjoy being at Al Lang Field in March. It was a good day we were having and I was happy he'd asked to come to the ballpark and watch the Rays.

No, that's a lie: In that last year of care, Dad never *asked* me for anything. I'd had to work through a backward conversation with him about spring training and getting him to a game. I'd had to beg, and then he'd finally agreed, though it was clear all along he was dying to go. Some complex combination of his aging, his personality and his status as a minor celebrity who'd spent a lifetime in baseball, left him incapable of polite requests— at least of me. I'd actually watched him struggle to say the word "please" to me, the spittle flying from his lips as he tried to utter it before giving up and issuing me a command. It was sometimes comic, often infuriating behavior and sadly pathetic thing to see, and I suspect he was as weirdly confused by his behavior as I was. Often, to avoid that struggle for politeness, he worked his way through a convoluted conversational gambit meant to finally lead *me* to ask *him* for whatever it was he wanted. He'd done it with his wife's health when she'd been struggling with her nicotine-gum

117

addiction and I'd sent that e-mail to my siblings about it. He'd done it any number of other times, too. For the trouble with his vision, for instance, I'd been visiting with the two of them in their two-bedroom apartment. Mom was off in her bedroom chewing her nicotine gum and lying on her back in bed, staring quietly at the ceiling. Dad sat in his wheelchair. I sat on the small couch near the living-room window where the eleventh-floor view of Boca Ciega Bay is impressive and off in the distance a line of hotels fronts the distant blues and greens of the Gulf of Mexico.

I commented on that splendid scene. "So, Dad, this is a hell of a view, isn't it?"

"I guess so."

"Boy, look at that. You can see for miles."

"Yeah, I guess you can."

"You want me to bring you over here so you can look out the window?"

"No, don't bother. I'm OK right here, where I can listen to the TV."

"Listen to the TV?"

"Yeah, I get a game on ESPN and listen to it."

"Listen to it?"

"Well, you know...."

"Know what? Can't you see that TV?"

"No, I can see it fine."

"You sure?"

"Well, yeah, I'm pretty sure."

"But maybe you'd like to see it a little better? And see the view out this window?"

"Well, yeah, I guess that'd be nice."

"So maybe we should get you some new glasses?"

"Well, now that you mention it, yeah, that'd be nice. Take me to an eyeglass place and get me some new glasses."

"Sure, Skip, no problem. Can I take you to the optometrist to get some new glasses, maybe this Friday, when I'm not teaching?"

I could hear the disappointment in his voice. "We could go now," he said.

"No," I said, "we can't go now. It's eight o'clock at night. The place is closed."

He stared at me, unhappy. "I'd like to go now."

"They're not open."

He accepted the news. "OK, Friday'll be fine. Pick me up about seven A.M."

118

"Seven? Dad, they're not even open then. How about ten?"

"No. Eight. Eight's OK. Get me at eight so we get there early."

"Dad, it's ten minutes from here. I'll make an appointment to get your eyes looked at and I'll let you know when. Let's aim at ten."

"Let's aim at eight."

I sighed. Dad's sense of time and the rest of the world's sense of time were not, I'd found, in the same ballpark. I wondered that day, not for the last time, if he'd always been this way. How did his players manage to get along with him in all his years of minor-league managing? Did the team bus always leave a couple of hours early? Did batting practice for a night game start at dawn?

When we took him to the optometrist (at ten A.M., much to his displeasure), we found out two things. First, his vision was in the range of 20–200, so he was, for all practical purposes, blind.

Second, cataracts were the culprit, and so new glasses weren't the answer, surgery was. He wanted the surgery on the spot. Now. But the optometrist, chuckling, explained it didn't work that way, and that he didn't do the surgery anyway.

Dad tried one more time. "Well, I'm here right now. You sure you can't do it?"

The optometrist smiled. "Yes, Mr. Wilber, I'm sure."

With the help of my mother-in-law, who'd been through cataract surgery herself, we found a good ophthalmologist—happily, a baseball fan—who spent the next eight weeks giving Dad back his sight, first in the right eye and then the left. It wasn't an easy process, dealing with Dad's attitude toward the surgery (he wanted it all done at once, and Now) or handling the flood of details from the pre-op to the operation to post-op for each eye. But we got it done and he could see again, his vision in the range of 20–50, a large improvement from where he'd been.

And now, here, at the ballpark, using those new eyes, he liked what he was looking at.

"That kid has a nice swing," he said of Ben Grieve.

I'm an amateur at swing analysis, but it was easy to agree. Grieve's swing is a smooth, flat arc that has just enough upward motion at the end to get the ball into the air. It has the look of a practiced swing, part natural art but mostly, I thought, the result of hard work. In that swing you can see the hours spent perfecting the motions that go into getting the bat to connect with the ball.

Still, despite the seeming perfection and a solid early career, Grieve's first season as a Devil Ray was a bust. He hit a disappointing .264 with just eleven home runs. I told Dad that, and mentioned that we were all hoping for more from Grieve this year.

Dad looked at me. "You know," he said, "his dad was my centerfielder."

"Grieve's dad played for you?"

"Yeah. Tom Grieve, when I managed at Denver."

I looked all this up later, at home. Ben's father, Tom Grieve, played nine seasons for the Senators, Rangers, Mets and Cardinals. In the minor leagues, he played for the Denver Bears in 1971 and 1972. Del Wilber managed the Bears those years. The 1971 team, in fact, finished 73–67 and won the American Association pennant.

Much later, Tom Grieve became general manager of the Texas Rangers, in one of those odd synchronicities that dot baseball everywhere. The Rangers are the team my father managed for that one game in 1973, sandwiched between Whitey Herzog's firing and Billy Martin's hiring. The Rangers won Dad's game, which makes Del Wilber the answer to a great trivia question: who is tied for the winningest manager in the history of Major-League Baseball, by percentage? Del Wilber: 1.000.

In my research I found a quote from Tom Grieve about his son: "As soon as he could walk I bought him one of those plastic whiffle bats and a balloon," the quote from BaseballLibrary.com goes. "It was pretty obvious at that young age that he had some ability."

The article added that as a high-school student, Ben Grieve hit .486 and his father used to take Ranger players, coaches and scouts to see his son play. Ben hung out in the clubhouse and dugout, too. The players "were pretty nice to me," Grieve was quoted during his rookie season.

That sounds familiar to me: the "pretty nice" players part if not the high-school batting average. With my brothers and sisters, I grew up surrounded by my father's friends, the other ballplayers, from the stars to the other journeymen like my father. In baseball's extended family, the players are famously nice to the kids. The memories of those days are everywhere for me, from running the bases in Fenway at age five while Ted Williams and Jimmy Piersall and Milt Bolling and Jackie Jensen and the other Sox waited near the cage to take batting practice; to Charleston, West Virginia, and my one summer as a batboy while Dad managed Triple A Senators to a losing season, but brought along players like Jim Kaat, Zoilo Versalles, Don Mincher, Jim Hall and others; to the time at age eighteen when Dad gave me (a college baseball player at the time for the University of Minnesota) that chance to pitch to Rod Carew in Bradenton, Florida's McKechnie field. The family spent time in Philly, in St. Louis, in Louisville, in Houston, in Chicago, in Boston. In all those places and others I got to know Dad's friends and colleagues, and they all treated me and my brothers and sisters like part of the family. Which is what we were. Which is, I suppose, even now what we still are.

In those days, I thought of Dad as about the most special father a boy could have. He was, in my eyes, not only a gifted athlete but a man of kindness, compassion and even a kind of genius. Once, in Charleston, in a high-powered negotiation with the previous season's batboy who held a job I badly wanted, Dad found a way to keep us both happy, sharing the job. My summer of being half-batboy for the Charleston Senators became one of the most enjoyable times of my childhood.

At Al Lang, sitting there in his wheelchair, just a few months from the end though we didn't know that for sure at the time, Dad told other stories, finding connections everywhere to the game as it used to be in simpler times. He remarked that Blue Jays manager Buck Martinez played for him in the minors, too. Martinez was fired by that June, but getting fired, Dad explained when Martinez was sent packing, was part of the deal, and that led him into the stories of his own firing, in Tacoma. He was drinking heavily in those days and that was his low-point, in baseball and perhaps in life and he never seemed to come fully out of the hole he'd dug for himself, though some years later he quit drinking when the doctors told him to. Later, he quit smoking, as well. In both cases, he did it cold turkey, with no help, no advice, no special plans. One day he drank and the next day he didn't. Same with cigarettes.

Every inning—no, every half inning, or even every at-bat at that spring-training game—there was another story to tell, some connection from this game and this place to a baseball history that went back more than a half-century. The joy I had in hearing those stories reminds me of two things: first, that major-league baseball is a tiny universe, where everyone knows everyone or everyone's children and grandchildren and so the stories thread seamlessly from one part of the extended family to the next.

Second, that baseball's power lies in its myth-making. It is the stories that emerge from baseball that hold our interest more than the games that are played. These stories often focus on singular moments of achievement or failure, with a Buckner error to balance every mythic Thomson home run.

The stories, in fact, almost always transcend statistics, bypassing the facts of careers for the more enjoyable folk tales, so that for a lot of men like my father, these moments more than outweigh mediocre careers. Three home runs in one game in Shibe Park in 1951, a single win as a big-league manager in 1973, a final professional home run in Louisville in 1959, a stand-in pose for a Norman Rockwell painting for a magazine cover in 1954, a tag on Yogi Berra at the plate in 1951—these moments and others and the stories behind them defined my father, they made him who he was. For better and, toward the end, for worse, when I discovered that some of his best stories were more myth than fact.

In this spring training game, in the middle of the fourth inning, with the Rays ahead one to nothing on a double by Steve Cox, the P.A. announcer said this: "Rays fans, in attendance today is a man who's spent fifty years in baseball. Please say hello to Del Wilber." Dad tried to stand and wave hello, this was something of a big moment for him. But the announcement was short and he moved very slowly and so he couldn't get more than halfway up from the chair before he ran out of energy and time and sat back down.

I'd hoped for more. The week before, as I was working through the media relations people for the Rays to arrange the day, my connection with the team had asked for a few lines about my father and I'd sent in this:

> In the stands today is Del Wilber, who recently moved from St. Louis to St. Petersburg. Del first came to Al Lang field for spring training in 1947. A catcher and pinch-hitter for the Cardinals, Phillies and Red Sox from 1946 to 1954, Del's baseball career spanned some fifty years as a player, a pennant-winning Triple-A manager, a scout for the Twins, Tigers and the A's, and a coach for the White Sox and the Washington Senators.

I'd hoped, especially, to get in the part about Dad's first visits to St. Pete for spring training. But perhaps it didn't matter, I thought, as the brief spatter of applause faded. The people around us recognized him, and Dad knew that the Rays, and by extension baseball itself, had said hello. For the third time in the day he smiled. Mom, confused, wondered why he'd tried to stand.

Dad wilted in the heat and humidity and so by the fifth inning I wheeled him out of the park and drove him and Mom back to the assisted-living place where they lived. My younger brother met us there and spent another hour or two with his parents. He's the general manager of a funny-car team in the NHRA circuit and he was in Gainesville that weekend for the Gatornationals. He drove the one hundred twenty miles or so south to St. Pete to be at the game and share the afternoon with his father and mother at the ballpark in the spring sunshine. His memories of Dad revolve firmly around baseball, so it was good that he made it to a spring-training game and shared that final bit of baseball with Dad, who would only last a few more months.

For me, I was pretty done with baseball by then and worn down by the craziness of caregiving for Dad and Mom, but the afternoon, I had to admit, had offered its own kind of perfection. For anyone who knows and loves baseball, major-league baseball in March in Florida is as good as it gets: smaller, mostly older and more intimate ballparks in the sunshine; a welcome informality from at least some of the players; a sense of the game as it used to be, back when five-thousand fans made for a pretty good crowd. So sitting with my father in Al Lang Field had carried me back warmly to those days in the 1950s when baseball, and spring training, was the focal point of the year for the Wilber family. God, those were wonderful days, back when baseball was the national pastime and my brothers and sisters and I got along pretty well, sharing our status as the children of a ballplayer and his beautiful wife. The truth in those days was so simple and so very understandable. I miss that uncomplicated clarity.

14

Alternate Realities

IN MY CHILDHOOD DAD WAS A DISTANT but much admired figure and it was Mom, always Mom, who was in charge. She was, I came to realize even in childhood, not much of a cook and an annoyingly heavy smoker; but those seemed her only failings. I think through my memories of my childhood and the only bad ones seem to center on food: nearly inedible tuna casserole on Friday nights for a good Catholic family; hard, dark hamburger patties or the occasional dried and tough steak and baked potato (my first good steak dinner, sometime in high-school at a downtown St. Louis restaurant, was a revelation to me); and always the cigarette in her fingers, held just so, the coquettish but deadly symbol of independence that had come to her through Dad's introduction during their wartime courtship. The smells I remember from growing up in St. Louis and other cities where we spent our summers are all warped by cigarette smoke. The stink of it was so constant and annoying (and dangerous, though we didn't know it then) that none of the five children of Del and Taffy Wilber became smokers.

But mostly the picture I hold in my mind from a childhood awash in sports in general and baseball in particular is one where Mom is behind the wheel taking me to practice, and it's Mom in the stands watching me play, and it's Mom helping me with my homework or, during our long weeks in spring training each year, teaching me from workbooks and textbooks so I'd be caught up when I returned to Mary, Queen of Peace School in Webster Groves, Missouri.

124

When I was in high school I benefited from Mom's work for the Cardinals, as did my brothers and sisters. We tend to make Dad the focus of our baseball memories, but it was Mom, in fact, who worked for the Cardinal front office for a good part of the 1960s and as part of her job package had four box seats to every Cardinal game. Those were good years for the Cardinals and we were there, the Wilber kids, hanging out in the front office at Busch Stadium, taking full advantage of our box seats during the pennant years of 1967 and 1968, watching Bob Gibson and Ken Boyer and Mike Shannon and the other Cardinals of that era.

We were pretty normal children, I would guess: better behaved than most, not prone to getting into trouble, not much into dabbling in drugs or alcohol. But I was never close to my older brother, who was a senior in high school when I entered as a freshman and so untouchably distant. He was also a far better student and athlete than me, so I spent four high-school years listening to teachers wonder what had gone so wrong with me that I couldn't measure up to my brother's perfection.

The older of my two sisters and I were close when we were young but drifted apart when she moved to California and I stayed in the Midwest. The younger of the two sisters and my younger brother were the babies of the family for a while and I was their brutal, nearly Dickensian, babysitter. As they grew up I became close for a time to my younger brother—we liked table hockey and played hard-fought games well into the night, using long-playing records as our time-keeper, the game ending with the final dying chords of the last song on each side. Then I moved to Florida more than twenty years ago and we went our separate ways.

Later, in adulthood, the younger of my two sisters went through a difficult divorce just a few years after I'd done the same. We were crucially important to each other's mental health there for a time and I owe her deeply for that. She helped raise my Down syndrome son, too, in the vital years after his mother left us. Even after I left for Florida and she happily remarried, we managed to stay close and she and her family often came to visit us in Florida and we, in turn, visited them in Illinois. We have a long, shared history together, more so than do most of the Wilber children.

But when it came to Mom and Dad, even sister Mary and I have our own separate memories, a past we have each woven of our father and our mother, as children must do, out of the cloth we were given, each of us creating our childhood from those things we were and saw and felt and learned growing up in the Midwest in a baseball town in a baseball family.

These personal histories are difficult to alter, so difficult that any attempt to do so provokes anger and disappointment, as I found in my troubled communication with my siblings not only during those months when I took care of Dad but also after his death. In some ways, in fact, the terrible friction that's come between us has enlarged since Dad died. They understandably choose to remember him in their own way and only grudgingly have they come to understand that I have to do the same. I can't pretend Dad's last months didn't happen. I can't pretend to not know the things I learned during that time.

In writing this book I have come to think of my father as a man of different versions to us all, depending on who you are and how you knew him. For my brothers there is Dad 1; the big-leaguer, the Triple-A manager, the coach, the scout, the storyteller. For one of my sisters there is Dad 2; the grandfather who doted on her children. For the other sister there is Dad 3; a man she struggled with some in her teenage years but came, ultimately, to admire, though she recognized his weaknesses as well as his strengths. For me there is Dad 4; the unhappy elderly man trapped in a body that disappointed him and trapped him with a son who disappointed him, as well.

Others outside the family saw even more versions of Del Wilber. My older brother, whose connection to professional sports is deep and long-term, seems in his travels to come across a steady stream of people who remember Del Wilber with fondness and admiration. And to Dad's friends in the town of Kirkwood who met him for breakfast several times a week and listened to him tell stories from baseball's golden era, he was the man who knew everyone who mattered in the game. To my wife's family he was the sad old man who'd played a game they didn't know or care about. To my daughter he was the difficult grandpa, while my father-in-law was, to her, the great grandpa.

To others he was others, garrulous and knowing, a heavy drinker and a smoker in the tradition of the ballplayers of his age, but a nice enough guy, and man with a certain skill at assessing talent as a scout and guiding its growth as a coach and manager.

A good friend of mine, author Jack McDevitt, sat next to me at an autographing table at a science-fiction convention a few years ago. The list of fans wanting me to sign books or copies of magazines I'd had a story in was a short one; the line for McDevitt, a major talent in the field, was long and demanding of his attention, but he took time out to chat with me and in the doing of that he asked me about my name. Was I related to Del Wilber, the old Phillies catcher?

I sighed. Here we go again. But I said yes, that old Philly was my father.

And McDevitt told me of the time when, growing up in the Philadelphia area, he'd been taken to a Phillies game by his father. They didn't have a lot of money and going was a rare treat. They got there early, managing to sneak down into the box seats and stand at the rail watching the players come out of the dugout to head out to the field to warm up. They yelled and pleaded for one player after another to come over and sign a scorecard and talk to a young boy who was a fan. But most of the Phillies, all but one of them, in fact, ignored them.

That one was Del Wilber, in the middle of his best single season of big-league ball, playing every day, hitting a few homeruns, making the plays at the plate: having a good season. Wilber came over to McDevitt and his dad and talked with them, signed the scorecard, chatted some more, said he had to go and went out to the field to loosen up.

Jack McDevitt never forgot that day, and as he told me the story at that convention I could see he was back in Philadelphia and he was ten years old again and Del Wilber was his favorite player. Jack wanted to know if he could meet Dad someday and I said I'd arrange it. Some months later when Dad was vacationing in St. Pete, Jack made the long drive down from his home in Georgia and met me and Dad for lunch.

I thought Dad would be happy to meet a fan from nearly fifty years before but he was strangely aloof and difficult. I didn't understand his attitude and had to push him to tell some of those great stories. Reluctantly, I thought, he did that, talking mostly about the Phillies in the early 1950s and what a great guy this player was and what a difficult one that one was. The hour passed quickly and we left. Later, I apologized to Jack. I'd had it wrong about Dad. I'd thought he'd love the chance to reminisce and to meet a well-known author in the bargain, but it didn't go the way I'd thought it would. Jack said he hadn't minded, that he'd met his boyhood hero, the player who'd talked to him in 1951, and that was all that mattered. Fair enough.

Another time I held a writers' spring training, bringing Jack and some other writer friends to town for a few days: the idea being we could do a little workshopping of each others' stories, and my friends—baseball fans, every one of them—could meet with Dad over dinner, chat with the old pro about the way it had really been, sit at his feet and hear the stories he loved to tell.

But here, too, he was difficult. He seemed reluctant and ill at ease. He spoke to groups all the time, always off-the-cuff and always full of memorable stories of the game in its glory. What happened to the gregarious storyteller? I didn't know. I still don't know.

15

Some Hard-Earned Advice

THE CHILDREN OF ELDERLY PARENTS in decline make excuses, especially in matters involving dementia. Dad's just tired. Mom's just confused.

This is understandable in several ways. It is hard for middle-aged children to accept the mortality of their parents with its underlying message about their own mortality. It is hard for grown children to accept that a necessary role reversal between parent and child has to take place. It is hard to accept that the parent or parents who were once the best possible source for all sorts of information now can't be trusted to balance a checkbook. It is hard to accept that the sweet-tempered grandfather or grandmother of recent years past has become a different person; sometimes an angrier, more demanding one.

All of this is hard to accept, but the caregiver quickly learns to face the facts as they are, not as he or she would wish them to be. Seeing Mom forget a conversation from five minutes ago, getting face to face with Dad's irrational anger and fear, listening to once-sweet Mom curse at you like a sailor: these things bring reality with them when they arrive.

It's the more distant children, the ones who come for occasional or even rare visits, the ones who get the news about Mom and Dad's struggles secondhand, who have the harder time accepting the changes. It is very easy, from a distance, to disbelieve the news one is hearing from a sibling who's the caregiver. Brother must be wrong about that. Sister is losing her patience, that's all. It can't be that bad. It can't be that hard. It can't be that wearing.

But it is, of course, all of those things: bad, hard, wearing, and more. And so a friction develops between the on-site caregiver and the more distant siblings. It takes a lot of communication, and just the right sort of communication, to ease that friction.

This is a lesson I learned much too late. The books I have read and the experts I have talked with since my father's death all offer good and useful advice and I just wish I'd had the sense to listen to that advice back when it really mattered, back when I might have made Dad and Mom—and myself—a little happier, and back when I might have headed off friction between the siblings. Instead, I muddled through, but at a cost higher than the one I might otherwise have had to pay in matters both small and large. On the small side, for instance, my lifetime habit of heavy reading nearly came to a halt. I went from one or two books a week to none for months at a time. More seriously, my writing dried up, too, from a daily goal of five hundred or a thousand words to a daily goal of typing a hurt or angry e-mail or two. Even more seriously, my teaching suffered. I didn't have the time, or the emotional wherewithal, to do the reading and grading that needed to be done, or to plan a decent lecture, or to meet with and advise students.

Most importantly, my family suffered. My temper was short and the time I spent with my son and daughter limited. Just as bad, the time I shared with my wife was not only curtailed by the demands of Dad and the needs of Mom, but also affected by my anger and frustration.

It wasn't a pleasant time. Like a lot of poorly prepared caregivers, I felt trapped and depressed. I felt like my siblings thought I was making it all up when I talked about Dad's behavior. I watched how he acted around them when they visited or when he got a phone call from one of them and I marveled at the changes in the man. Why couldn't he be half that nice to me? Why had he become, for me, the often insufferable man he'd become? Why couldn't he even say "please" to me?

I didn't have any answers to these questions and I was too busy, too frustrated, too depressed, too caught up in emotional survival to go find the answers somewhere. Only now, long after the fact, have I come to realize that help was out there in several forms and I should have found it and asked, even begged, for support. I would have been much better off, certainly, if I had done so. And, most importantly, Dad and Mom would have been much better off, too: happier, calmer, more rational.

But I learned this much too late. I'd been a reasonably competent guy all my life; I'd raised a special-needs child, I was a good parent (or trying hard to be) to a bubbly, energetic bright young girl. I was a good husband and a half decent provider. I felt like a good partner in life with my wife. I felt like I had things under control. After all, though in my fifties I could still throw a baseball and make it curve, I could hit a three-point jumper on the local basketball courts, ride my bicycle for fifteen miles at a time then jog a couple more. I read voraciously, I enjoyed arguing politics with my conservative colleagues. I enjoyed, in fact, generally. Life was pretty damn good.

But I couldn't handle the caregiver role. At best, I could survive it (and one dark day even that was in question). So here's my hard-earned advice for every caregiver to come: prepare for the caregiver role by learning about it before you take it on; admit your limitations; assume the worst while hoping for the best; know your siblings will likely not understand what you're going through; get professional help from the start if you can afford it. In fact, get professional help from the start even if you can't afford it. And save yourself before you save your mother or father or both. Remember that when you are drowning, your parents are drowning with you, whether they realize it or not.

Recognizing and accepting the caregiver role seems to me to be a crucial first step toward achieving the best possible physical and emotional health for both the care recipient and the caregiver. Often, the adult child of an elderly parent or parents falls into the caregiver role without an adequate understanding of, or preparation for, the challenges that he or she will face as a caregiver.

"Caregiver" has several definitions. In its original coinage, the term referred to health care professionals, either those working in a health-care facility or, often, those paid to live in or regularly visit the home of someone needing professional assistance. Over time, "caregiver" came to include in-home non-paid family members. More recently, the term has broadened to include all those (usually family members) who give care to those with special needs. In terms of elderly parents, according to one agency on aging, a caregiver is one who "provides unpaid assistance to a spouse, relative, or friend who is ill, disabled, or needs help with basic activities or daily living. Do you help with rides to the doctor, shopping, meals, bill paying, bathing, grooming, dressing, walking or transferring to a wheelchair, housekeeping, managing medications, or arranging services to be provided by others? If you provide services like these, whether or not you live with the person you are helping, you are a caregiver.*

The Family Caregiver Alliance defines a caregiver as "...anyone who provides basic assistance and care for someone who is frail, disabled or ill and needs help.† FCA adds that "Caregivers perform a wide variety of tasks to assist someone else in his or her daily life, for example, balancing a checkbook, grocery shopping, assisting with doctor's appointments, giving medications, or helping someone to eat, take a bath or dress. Many family members and friends do not consider such assistance and care 'caregiving'—they are just doing what comes naturally to them: taking care of someone they love. But that care may be required for months or years, and may take an emotional, physical and financial toll on caregiving families."

One particularly useful definition comes from Thomas Day,‡ director of the National Care Planning Council and chief spokesperson for the Utah Elder Care Planning Council. Day distinguishes between formal caregivers (paid professionals) and informal caregivers. "Informal caregivers," he says, "are family, friends, neighbors or church members who provide unpaid care out of love, respect, obligation or friendship to a disabled person. These people far outnumber formal caregivers and without them, this country would have a difficult time formally funding the caregiving needs of a growing number of disabled recipients."

Day adds that "About two-thirds of those (informal) caregivers ... are employed full-time or part-time, and two-thirds of those—about 45 percent working caregivers (overall)—report having to rearrange their work schedule, decrease their hours or take an unpaid leave in order to meet their caregiving responsibilities."

AARP defines "caregivers" as those who give assistance to another adult who is ill, disabled or otherwise needs help. AARP notes that while each caregiver's experience is unique, some common challenges that caregivers face are these:**

---

*Area Agency on Aging, Pasco-Pinellas (Florida): http://www.agingcarefl.org/caregiver/caregiver

†Family Caregiver Alliance:http://caregiver.org/caregiver/jsp/content_node.jsp?nodeid=392

‡Thomas Day, Guide to Long Term Care Planning: http://www.longtermcarelink.net/eldercare.htm

**AARP website: http://www.aarp.org/families/caregiving/caring_help/a2003–10–27-caregiving-newcaregiving.html

- Less time for personal and family life. Caregiving takes time. As a result, caregivers have less time to spend with other family members or less leisure time for themselves.
- The need to balance job and caregiving responsibilities. Caregiving tasks—such as taking your father to the doctor, or talking to a social worker about community services—usually must be done during work hours. This can present problems on the job.
- Financial hardships. The products and services associated with providing care can be costly. Those costs can quickly add up.
- Physical and emotional stress. Caregiving can be physically and emotionally stressful, especially for those providing intense levels of care for long periods of time.

As a result of facing these challenges, some caregivers, especially those who (like myself) are inadequately prepared for the hard work or struggle to accept their limitations in terms of time, organizational skills or the inevitable emotional turmoil, find themselves falling into a state of depression that begs for professional help. In the on-line article "Caregiving Guilt Can Be Tempered by Support System,"* writer Beth Witrogen McLeod notes that "some 52 million Americans care for a disabled or sick family member, according to a 1999 survey conducted by the U.S. Department of Health and Human Services. And although most bear their burden with love, social workers say caregiving is so demanding that most people feel inadequate." McLeod adds wisely that caregivers need to beware of guilt, because (as many caregivers learn the hard way), "Eventually, such emotions can extract a heavy toll on the health of the caregiver—and that hurts everyone involved."

There are a number of immensely useful books that any caregiver should be familiar with before taking on the role. If the job comes up on you too suddenly to allow for a careful read beforehand, then you will want to get a few of these books early on and read through them as issues arise. And they will arise. From the more than fifty books I read after the fact as part of the research for this book, I have culled a dozen of the ones that served me best and you can find that list in the "Some Useful Resources" appendix at the back of this book.

Some of the material in these books is downright angry, stories written by the exasperated adult children of elderly parents. The pain and anger of these writers is something I'm sympathetic toward, and I recognize my

*2000 Healtheon/WebMD.

133

father and my mother in the stories the writers tell of their parents. I see myself in the worn-down, depressed adult children who struggle so with the demands of the caregiving job. It is helpful, in fact, to know that my struggles weren't unusual or solely mine.

But anger and depression aren't particularly useful for anyone, other than as a way to recognize that the caregiving role is a difficult one and has its repercussions in multiple generations of a family. In my case, Dad has been dead for several years now and yet he still controls his children, his behaviors during that final year or so of his life still separating us. Some of my siblings remember one man; I remember another. I've tried to reconcile those two versions and asked them to do the same, but it's hard for them to really understand what caregiving is like. Some of my siblings seem able to recognize the validity of both perspectives, but for others, that's harder to do. Even in death my father remains the sun of our familial solar system and all five of his children remain firmly in his orbit in one way or another.

Other books are less angry and more thoughtful. From these the three most useful from my worn-out caregiver's point of view are the excellent and informative *Are Your Parents Driving You Crazy*, by Joseph A. Ilardo and Carole R. Rothman; the extremely useful *Coping with Your Difficult Older Parent*, by Grace Lebow and Barbara Kane, with Irwin Lebow; and the powerful and illuminating *Necessary Losses*, a classic from the mid–1980s by Judith Viorst.

Viorst's book reminds me, for instance, that Dad bears a good part of the responsibility for the man he was toward the end. After all, Viorst says, "Old age is our responsibility too. Indeed, it has been argued that healthy-enough older people should not be exempt from the judgments of the world, and that if they are boring, garrulous, self-centered, vapid, querulous or obsessed with the state of their belly and their bowels, we sometimes ought to say to them, "Shape up!'"*

Even more importantly, I learn from Viorst that when it comes to answering the question about whether rivalries like those I've had with my siblings are universal and normal, the answer is that "Ten out of ten psychoanalysts answer yes. And while it may be more intense in firstborn children, or between two children (or more) of the same sex, or when the children are fairly close in age, or when the families are smaller rather

Viorst, Necessary Losses, *pp. 297–298.*

134

than larger, it is doubtful that any one of us is untouched by these rivalrous feelings, is wholly exempt."

Viorst, quoting another source, adds that "Sibling rivalries remain a secret, a shameful secret, a dirty little secret. And this secrecy ... can help perpetuate the sibling rivalry. Thus many brothers and sisters will remain ferocious rivals all their lives. They never let go of their jealousy and competitiveness. And in spite of everything else that may be happening to them elsewhere, they remain intensely embroiled with one another."

And finally, she notes this, which struck home with me as I thought through the unfortunate truth that I've never been more distant from my brothers than I am now, in the years following our father's death: "Psychologist Robert White, discussing sibling conflicts that have not been resolved during childhood, says that adult sibling rivals are still competing 'for the favor of parents who might be aged, senile or even dead.'"*

I read that, and the rest of Viorst's thoughts on life's losses, and I think yes, and yes, and yes again, page after page. Then I think through the troubles I'm having with all of my siblings and I ask myself whose fault this is, who's guilty?

And I realize that asking the question points an arrow at the problem. No one's guilty, it's no one's fault: and we're all guilty and at fault, as well. We're adults, damn it, and we ought to be able to give and take, to work through the troubles, to reconcile. As Viorst says, "Even when rivalries continue into adult life, change and reconciliation are possible. Old patterns persist but are not carved in stone.... And sometimes a family crisis can bring siblings closer. Insight at any age into our hurtful repetitions may free us to do it differently at last. It need not always be the way it was.

"This sharing, if we are able to get past the rivalry, can lay the foundation of a lifetime connection, a connection that can sustain us though parents die and children leave and marriages fail. For while brothers and sisters mean loss—the loss of our mother's (or father's) exclusive love—that loss can yield immeasurable gain."†

As I pull Lebow's *Coping* book down from the shelf and take a look at it again I see page-corners turned down; I see underlined passages on nearly half the pages; I see exclamation points where a sentence or two par-

*Viorst, Necessary Losses, pp. 94–96.
†Viorst, Necessary Losses, pp. 98–99.

ticularly struck home; I see scribbled-in comments like "Skip Keeping Score," and "Big Lies," and "Stress and Depression."

Working my way through this book in a quick replay of the days I spent reading it after Dad's death (too late for it to help, alas), I take the opening "Difficult Parent Questionnaire," which starts with Dependency Behaviors, then moves to Turnoff Behaviors, Self-centered Behaviors, Controlling Behaviors, Self-destructive Behaviors, and then Fearfulness Behaviors.

The first question in Dependency Behaviors is "Your Parent Wants You All the Time." I put a check mark next to that. No, I put two checkmarks. In the months I spent as Dad's caregiver I rarely had a day go by when I didn't get a phone call with one demand or another.

I also put a check mark by "Makes Unreasonable and Irrational Demands," and another by "Attaches Himself to Another Person, Leaning on That Person for Everything," and then I move on to the next category, Turnoff Behaviors. Checkmarks there go next to "is tactless," and "has temper tantrums, e.g., throws things, or uses abusive language" (though I'm thinking of Mom when I check that one, and not poor Dad, who was the target of much of Mom's behavior).

I move on to Self-Centered Behaviors and here I check four of the five: "has a distorted self-image, viewing self as 'something special...'"; "interprets events solely as to how they affect him ... oblivious to the effect on others"; "guards his own turf," "is jealous of others."

Controlling Behaviors is the next category and I check off two; "manipulates others by the use of such techniques as guilt and flattery" and "makes demands so excessive that the opposite is achieved."

Self-destructive Behaviors is next, and Dad gets a clean bill there, avoiding or shedding his addictions, never struggling with compulsive behaviors other than his penchant for storytelling, never destructively masochistic or suicidal.

We're on a roll, since Dad slides right by the entire next category, too, since I saw no problems at all with "Fearfulness Behaviors." He dodged nicely past any panic attacks, phobias, or the expectation of magical cures (though I nearly check that one, and would, except that his optimism over various miracle drugs turned out to be quite right once or twice. It's hard to argue with success).

That's it, and so, whew, I think as I look back at all these things I marked off; yes, these issues pretty much sum up the old pro in that last year.

And then, just three pages later I read this: "If you focus solely on your parent's problem behaviors and not the relationship between the two of you, chances are you will get nowhere."

And a light bulb clicks on for me. We had two different ideas of what was going on in those last months, Dad and I. We lived in two different worlds. His world was filled with limitations; constricted and lonely and demanding in ways that he'd never encountered before. My world was nearly the opposite; open and interesting and full of promise. I had a publisher for my novel, a publisher for my textbook, a long and solid teaching career, two wonderful and happy children, a lovely and intelligent wife. Hell, I even had a baseball team that was filled with players old enough and slow enough that I could play at their level. Life for me was pretty good. Life for Dad was pretty wretched.

And yet we had to get along. We had to work together. We had to find ways to meet his needs and Mom's without completely constricting mine.

But that was selfish of me, and frankly not possible. Something had to give and it had to be me. He was old and dying. Mom was incapable of helping him as she slipped ever deeper into her cognitive fog. I had to step up to the plate (a metaphor he would have loved) and get it done. A little constriction here and there, or even a lot of constriction here and there, was a small enough price to pay to honor my father and mother.

But that was hard to see from where I stood at the time. Part of me recognized the situation and my sister Cindy, in particular, helped me to understand that my perception of my father was particular to the relationship I had with Dad and that not only was his relationship with my siblings better, even his comments about me to the others were kinder, more considerate, more thoughtful, than anything he could ever say to my face.

But I was caught up in the day-to-day struggle, trying to survive the relationship's difficulties and too filled with anger and frustration to worry about anything larger. At one point, Cindy wrote me a kind and thoughtful and supportive e-mail. She was trying to prop me up a bit in my struggles. She told me that my father loved and respected me in his own way, and that he was appreciative of what I was doing for him. But I, alas, was having none of it, and replied with this:

Subject: Skip
Date: 13 May 2002
From: Rick Wilber

...as to Skip: He usually treats me like shit, no matter what he says to you or Mary. He needs to command, and I'm the only one around to do that with, so he does. As I said in one post, I recognize what's happening, how his world has narrowed and commanding me is probably helping to keep him alive and sane. I try to just sigh. I try to just laugh it off. But every now and then it's just way over the top, and yesterday was one of those days. Please understand that yesterday was excessive but it's—always—like that from him to me. He'll be better now for a few days, and he's very penitent at the moment. But give him a little time and he'll be back at it.

And I'll say again that his inability to politely ask for anything is incredibly annoying. Clearly he finds being polite to be demeaning and beneath him—he did, after all, hit three homeruns in one game in 1951 and, to his mind, sometimes I forget that earned him emperor status forever. He'd rather knowingly treat me like shit than be even marginally polite. He admitted as much to me yesterday, and said he was sorry about it. To his credit, it's 9:30 and he hasn't called yet today.

—Rick

In other words, after a single year of caregiving for my parents, I'd lost just about every bit of the patience and understanding that I'd once had. I knew it, too, as the e-mail makes clear; but knowing it didn't matter. The well was dry. The man was dying and I knew it and yet I behaved like that.

What could I have done? What should I have done? With my ailing parents? With my siblings? Two years too late I asked that of Grace Lebow, co-author of the *Coping with Your Difficult Older Parent,* book. In one telephone interview of less than an hour's length and through several subsequent e-mails I struggled to understand my failings and put them into some sort of perspective. Lebow is a clinical social worker and a care manager (a term I wish I'd been familiar with during my tour of duty as my father's caregiver). Co-founder (with Barbara Kane) of Aging Network Services in Bethesda, Maryland, her job is to help caregivers do two important things: take care of their elderly charges and take care of themselves.

Lebow has pretty much seen it all, and in talking to her and reading her book I came to realize that what I thought was special about myself, my father, and my situation wasn't that special at all. Yes, Dad had been a professional baseball player and coach. Yes, he'd led an interesting life. Yes, he'd been a good, if often absent, father. Yes, he'd become unhappy and demanding in his final months. Yes, he'd been rough on his caregiver and nicer, even sweet and gracious, to his other sons and this eventually caused some serious rifts between myself and my brothers. But all of that, except for the baseball, can be part of the package for any adult child who is the caregiver for an elderly parent. The sub-title for Lebow's book, after all, is *A Guide for Stressed-Out Adult Children.*

Lebow helped me see that the problems I faced with my father and mother began with our decision to move them from St. Louis to St. Petersburg. A move from one city to another might be made with the best of intentions, Lebow pointed out, but it is, after all, "a major life change. It's traumatic even if the person wants to move and is eager to move."

In my case, my mother had wanted to move to Florida for many years but Dad had always resisted. In St. Louis he was something of a minor institution in that most baseball of cities. He often spoke to groups, sharing stories of the game in its glory days. He was part of the locally famous 1-2-3 Club, a group of mostly older sports figures in the city. He was an ex–Cardinal and the center of attention at the regular breakfast gatherings in the drugstore diner in his small suburban town of Kirkwood. The locals loved the old ballplayer.

And yet we moved him to St. Petersburg, taking him from his home of fifty years and all the relationships that came with that, and placed him and his wife into an assisted-living facility that could take care of their physical needs but couldn't help much, it turned out, with their emotional ones.

It's terribly hard, Lebow noted. "Children come to us and ask 'How do I get my parents to agree to move closer to me?' And I tell them it's a high-risk situation and you have to weigh the relative risks of what can happen in a move to the risks of remaining where they are."

We didn't much weigh the risk, we just seized the moment. Was Dad apprehensive about the move? He didn't say so. Plus, we figured, he had a certain comfort zone with the St. Petersburg area and Florida's West Coast. He'd spent a month or more at a time nearly every year since before World War II here, either at spring training or, later in his career, managing in the Fall Instructional League, a job he held for many years beginning in the 1960s. There he had a hand in working with promising young talent like the Twins' Tony Oliva and also with established players who wanted to work on something particular, perhaps a change in position, as happened in 1968 with Rod Carew.

But we figured wrong and St. Petersburg wasn't St. Louis. There was no special club just for guys like him. There was no group of local admirers listening again and again to his stories over breakfast, though there was that men's group that gets together to talk sports. For reasons I didn't understand, Dad wasn't interested in attending those meetings. Pride? I suppose so.

When I talked about all this with Lebow, wondering if the move was the right thing to do, she said, cautiously, "Well, that's the question that people have to ask. You have to really weigh that. The (St. Louis) community knew him and people could visit him there. His spirits might have been better there." I got the message. Unknowingly, we set a trap for the old pro. My siblings and I set him up to be unhappy.

After the move, when the emotional tangles started to grow and engulf me, I could and should have sought advice. As the child-in-charge I was not only struggling with my parents, I was inadvertently building walls between myself and my siblings, and especially my brothers, as each hard week went by. When I told Lebow of this she wasn't surprised. Lebow is a care manager, the term given to those who become middlemen in the sometimes agonizing process of handling the lives of elderly parents with dignity. When there are multiple children, she says, "It's usually those children who want help and not the parents."

What the care manager can provide is a certain neutrality, an emotional distance from the issues at hand, that allows for decision making that isn't marred by the turmoil that can swirl around siblings with varied abilities and goals. "Distance is what care managers provide all over the country," she said. "We're able to talk to the children and get everybody's viewpoints. We'll get one son or daughter in the office and get everyone on the conference call at the same time so we could all speak together. That's important, that everyone is on the same line and pulling together."

That's easier said than done, of course, and even when it works it doesn't solve all the problems, but, as Lebow says, at least if there are disagreements the children can talk it out, and even when the children are in full agreement a neutral care manager can point out problems that the children just can't see, including the merits or problem with their group communication with their elderly parents.

"In your particular case," she told me, "we might have used baseball as a tool to talk with your dad, build some communication, and then introduce him to someone who could help him with his wife."

Lebow has seen it often, of course. She guessed how Dad's thinking might have gone when he took some of the actions that he took, and what a care manager might have done to help: "He's thinking, 'I'm worried about my wife, I'm worried about myself,' and it would be our job to figure out what words to use that are not objectionable to him to get in the door and start to help him. That's basically where you have to start, on his turf, talking with him about a way to help him."

It just might have worked, I thought, as Lebow explained how the care manager helps arrange for a social worker to be in touch with elderly parents. What a concept! A social worker, I thought, could have taken heat even if the plan wasn't working all that well. I said this to Lebow and she responded: "Well, yes, you wouldn't be the one getting all those calls. The social worker would be getting them and handling them. She would e-mail everyone so that one person in the family didn't have to shoulder it all. You'd still have the basic responsibility but you'd have the help you need."

Sometimes, Lebow added, the care manager will bring in a private caregiver for extra help. In my father's situation, for instance, if Dad felt the assisted-living facility wasn't doing enough for him, the social worker could have helped steer me toward the right person and hire that person and interview that person.

Would that have helped? Perhaps. At the time I felt that I was trapped between the rock of a spoiled, demanding father and the hard place of an angry, addicted mother in the early throes of Alzheimer's. One more layer, a neutral person whom Dad didn't see in the same light in which he saw me, might well have eased the daily stresses considerably.

This help doesn't come cheaply, of course. Lebow notes that "It's all privately paid, Medicare doesn't touch this at all." But remember that the difficulties run through the whole family, and so Lebow's advice is for the family, not just the parents, to pay for a care manager's services. Typically, the fees start with an initial family consultation that runs about $350 and gets the basics underway, including a social worker. After that, the social worker will have his or her own fees, ranging from eighty to more than one hundred thirty dollars an hour for home visits.

Once the program is in place, the social worker (or an assistant), can help when and wherever needed: taking Dad to the doctor, for instance. Lebow stressed to me that the most important thing is for adult children of elderly parents to give it some considerable thought beforehand, to be prepared.

"There are things that most [adult children] people need to pay attention to, but most don't. That starts with talking with your parents, opening up the communication about their fears about getting older, their worries. Most parents are willing to talk to their children about this, but most children are hesitant to bring up the subject.

"Sometimes it's the parents who don't want to discuss it—they are in denial, [saying] 'I'm never going to get old and let's not talk about this.' But still, give them the opportunity and [you'll find] that there are things they may let their children know; financial things, advance directives, anything they're willing to talk about. Then, if you keep that communication open and start it early, it's easier to open up the subject again and again."

When it comes to the caregiver and his or her siblings, it's crucial, Lebow said, to realize that typically all the siblings want to feel they are making a contribution and so it's good for the caregiver to find ways to have them help out with caregiving. Telephone calls, cards and flowers, expert advice on financial issues; all are helpful.

In my case, I sent those daily e-mails to my four siblings, detailing how it was all going and, occasionally, asking for help. Were the e-mails a good idea? At the time I certainly thought so. When the pressure from Dad became too much I would ask my siblings to call him on the telephone and take the pressure off me some. They always did and, usually, Dad would back off for a while. That seemed a productive use of e-mail.

But there were many more times when I used the e-mails simply to vent my own frustrations and anger and general unhappiness. Too often, I think, I talked about the difficulties, and not often enough, perhaps, did I talk about the positives. Ultimately, this cost me, and today I am a great deal more estranged from my siblings than I would be had I not been so honest, so emotional, even so venomous, in my e-mails.

When I asked Lebow about the e-mails she responded more positively than I'd guessed she would. "I think that what you did sounds excellent and you got results from it. You took advantage of communication in the digital age. E-mail can be terrific."

But hadn't my e-mails been ultimately counterproductive? "That's not what you meant to do, but they might have seemed that way to your brothers and sisters," she said. "But I still think it's better that they have information rather than no information. You might have said something about that, saying this is not what I meant to do. I think that's hard, though, because you did need the support."

One important thing that might have helped us all enormously would have been a get-together, a more formal meeting to talk things through and plan ahead. "It's very useful if the siblings are willing to come together, to come to one spot and be together on an occasional basis with the plan of helping the caregiver and giving support to the caregiver; and I don't mean financial support, I mean, for the caregiver to say 'I need you guys. I need everyone to come and give me a boost.'"

Ironically, the one single time we all got together for just such a meeting was at Dad's funeral service. That, of course, was too little and very much too late and I found myself the outsider—an alien among my own brothers and sisters—at that dinner and at a similar one that took place some months later. They were chatty and full of those good memories they had from Dad's better days. I was in a far darker mood and resented that they did not want to hear what I had to say. I felt like my hard work was not only unacknowledged but resented by several of them. I'd learned things they emphatically did not want to know and I resented their pretense. I felt like I had earned the right to speak the truth as I knew it, and the least they could have done was listen and commiserate a bit before going back to their warm memories. Dad had treated them differently, which is part of the package that a caregiver buys when he or she takes on the job. I knew that. But I knew, too, that he'd been a sweetheart with them and then turned around and been the demanding and disappointed man he'd been with me. Their acknowledgment of my reality would have helped a lot; but they just did not see it that way and were angry with me when I did. So I held it in, where it bubbled for a long, long time. Where, perhaps, some of that resentment bubbles still.

These various kinds of siblings issues are common. Lebow and every expert I talked to and every book I read on the subject of caregiving touched upon that at some point. Sometimes, Lebow said, the problems are like mine, where the caregiver says, "Oh, if only I was alone I could do something and get some action here without [worrying over] all these sensitivities." But at other times, she said, "People would come to us and say, 'Oh, if only I had siblings this would make all the difference in the world.'"

The trick, of course, is for the caregiver to find a sense of balance in order to keep the teeter-totter of sibling rivalries perfectly poised, both sides at an even level. But that's damn hard, and when you're the caregiver you have other, more pressing matters, to fret over. Having to factor in sibling sensitivities just adds one more thing to worry about. As Lebow points out, "You can only handle so much. And the siblings are handling things too, and it's hard for them, too. They do often feel guilty. They feel that they're not doing the main thing for their parents."

So what's to do? I think about that article in *Time* magazine that talks about "simmering resentment re-erupting" and I worry that caregiving and sibling harmony don't seem to go together. When I was hard at the task I tried the wringing of the hands response and that didn't work. I tried bottling it up inside and that worked for my brothers (I was open and honest with my sisters) but most definitely that didn't work for me. I had no answers.

Stupidly, many months after my father's death but during a time when I definitely wasn't yet over the hard times, I tried the "My memories versus yours" technique when the siblings would send around group e-mails of some glowing memory of baseball in the old days and how great Dad had been in various ways. They would send those around and I would just shake my head in dismay and respond with a comment on the man I'd known in his final months; on the demands and the anger and the fear. They didn't like hearing that. I don't blame them.

Dad's problems were compounded by the failing mind of his wife of more than fifty years. I'm sure he must have felt that she wasn't living up to her part of the bargain they'd struck back in 1943. He'd be the ballplayer and she'd be the baseball wife. Now, when he needed her the most, she just wasn't capable of it.

One warm late-summer evening my wife and I took Mom and Dad to our daughter's soccer practice. By then I'd taken Mom to the neurologist a few times and we'd begun to explore the cause of her troubles. The neurologist, Dr. Dan Bell, is the same doctor who later diagnosed Dad with Parkinson's and got him on medication that brought the Parkinson's under control. Like all of Dad's doctors, Bell was a baseball fan. He had Missouri connections, as well, and was always happy to engage Dad in conversations about the Cardinals.

Bell suspected Alzheimer's was the cause of my mother's troubles, but there were still other possible causes, too, it seemed early on. Whatever the cause, her behavior was erratic, her short-term memory failing fast, and her needs beginning to mount. Dad didn't want to admit that, but I knew it was time we talked it over. So my wife took Mom over to get a closer look at her granddaughter's soccer skills so I could have a few words privately with Dad.

"You know, Taffy's mind isn't as sharp as it used to be, Skip," I said. "She can't remember much."

"You got that right," he grumbled.

"The doc says it might be Alzheimer's. It might be something else, but it might be Alzheimer's."

"Alzheimer's, that's when you get stiff," he said.

I smiled. "That's arthritis you're thinking of, Dad. Alzheimer's is a mental thing. It has to do with memory."

He didn't say anything.

"So here's the deal," I said. "You're going to have to be the brains of the outfit. Your mind is sharp. You're as smart as ever. You're going to have do the thinking for both of you."

He didn't say anything, but just stared at me. He very much did not *want* to be the brains of the outfit, that was clear. He'd spent a lifetime being taken care of by his wife and now I was telling him, even as his own body was failing him, even as his need for help was escalating, that she couldn't do that anymore. It must have seemed like she was abandoning him at his hour of greatest need. Even worse, right when he needed and wanted help he was being told instead that a role reversal was in the offing: he'd have to help her instead of her helping him. That must have seemed absolutely absurd to him. I'm guessing that it must have sounded like I was asking him to do the impossible. He'd mostly chosen not to take care of these things himself over the years, anyway; but his new set of physical limitations made certain that he simply couldn't—not just wouldn't—do things for himself and now I was saying that not only must he start doing fending for himself, he also had to help his wife along her own difficult path. Not surprisingly, the idea didn't go over too well and a few months later it became that major flashpoint in the relationship between Dad, Mom and me, when his concern over his own care outweighed his concern for her health and I reacted so badly to his misbehavior.

Some months after Dad died, and long after we were more certain of Mom's Alzheimer's diagnosis, I talked with the two doctors who knew them best during their time in St. Petersburg, Dr. Dan Bell (the neurologist) and Dr. Joe Springle (the primary care physician). I wanted to know how common my parents' emotional troubles had been, and what I could and should have done better to help get Dad and Mom through those hard times.

"These are hard things to go through [for the elderly]," Springle said when we met in a local restaurant and talked it over. "In your Dad's case, it must have been difficult to be an athlete and have a lot of self esteem wrapped up in your ability to do certain things and then that skill goes away."

We talked of their addictions, the smoking and the drinking, and how they'd mostly broken free of those late in life and shared a number of good years together as grandparents and retirees. We talked, too, about Dad's cancer and his stoic disregard toward what I had guessed must have been terrible pain. But that, said Springle, is a common misconception about cancer. "There's this belief that cancer is equated with pain and that you're going to have pain," he said, "but about half of cancer patients have mild pain at worst and the others have pain that can be well controlled."

That was a relief. Dad had said he had very little pain, even when the cancer was eating away at his spine; but I thought all along that there must have been considerable pain and he'd been hiding it.

It turns out that's hard to do. As Springle said, "It's hard to mask pain. You can say you don't have pain but it's obvious to others that you do, so it's very likely that he didn't have a lot of pain. You can look at the person and if they're wincing you know that the words don't ring true with what your seeing, so that's perfectly reasonable that that was the case with him."

I asked him, too, about Dad's attitude, that thing I had struggled with the most. Was his behavior, I wondered, tied tightly into his physical decline? Had he become this newly angry and demanding person in response to a body that was letting him down?

It's not simple as that, of course. Springle explained that "Even when you have medical difficulties the great part of [your behavior] is what you bring to the table; but when you're stressed some of your personality characteristics can seem magnified. In my practice I never see somebody who's 180 degrees away from who they were; but I do see some of their traits get magnified."

We talked about Dad's demands—the bacon cheeseburgers from Wendy's or adult diapers from Walgreens—that came even when he wasn't hungry or had a closet full of those same diapers. Springle, who saw Dad in full form several times in the examining room, with that right arm raised for immediate attention, like an earnest fourth-grader in the front row of the class, said, "I would describe your dad as someone who was the king [in his family]," he said, "and while you weren't as used to that role as your mom was, you probably played that role when you were young before you moved away and he was used to seeing you doing that."

I brought up other unpleasant surprises, too, like the times when Dad and Mom both had surprised me with remarks that were rude or even, one or two notable times, racist. I wondered if this was a social façade falling away. Were the remarks about my African-American friends' new baby some sort of window into a darker soul for Dad, for Mom?

146

Well, no. Springle made it clear I was doing Dad and Mom both a disservice by paying too much attention to those moments. "If your memory of them is not filled with that, I'd be more inclined to think of them the way they were for most of their lives," he said. "Remember, your dad was stressed. Under those conditions sometimes you say bizarre things you'd never say otherwise.

"Remember, too, that your mom had always been his caregiver, for his whole life, and then not only was she not taking care of him, she was hitting him." This violence under such trying circumstances, he said, had to raise the stress levels on Dad up to, and beyond, the breaking point. "It was hard enough for him to put up with losing her as caregiver," Springle noted, "but to actually have her become violent toward him, that must have been very hard."

A week later, over a few cups of coffee at the same restaurant, Dr. Dan Bell had much the same sort of information to share with me.

When it came to my mother's slide into dementia, he talked about how common her memory loss is and that he sees it every day. But he added that it isn't always, or even often, Alzheimer's that's causing the troubles.

The causes of memory loss are all over the place, he said, and "The first thing we do is look for something treatable that can be reversed. So we look for medications, for instance, as the number one. Then we look to see if [the patient] is depressed, that's another common cause of memory loss."

Depression can be treated. "Zoloft, Paxal, Prozac, they're all in the same category and work in the same fashion. They work on producing seratonin, a chemical in the brain that when it's depleted can lead to depression."

There is no test yet for Alzheimer's since there are no good chemical markers for it, so, says Bell, "When we first see someone we don't say they have dementia, we say, well, we've got some tests we want to run. We look and see if there is something metabolic going on, a thyroid disorder, a B-12 deficiency, maybe. We even screen them for syphilis, which is something we see a couple of times a year and it's something that you can totally treat with an antibiotic and the patient oftentimes returns to normal.

"A lot of it depends on what the story is," he adds. "If it's something that seems really recent, that seems like sudden changes, than sometimes we'll do a blood-work and make sure they didn't have a stroke, or have a tumor. Urinary tract infections are very common in older patients, too, and are really a common cause for a person to start declining. They don't get a burning, they don't get a fever, so it can be hard to find; but it's probably one of the most common causes of memory loss. We prescribe a round of antibiotics for a week and that will usually clear that up and you'll see improvement."

The diagnosis of Alzheimer's, Bell notes, is not nearly so common as the public thinks. "Really when you first see someone it's about fifty-fifty that it will be something reversible."

In my mother's case, the strange addiction to nicotine was unusual, but he does see elderly patients who abuse other stimulants. "I've had some patients who got into the habit and they drink two or three pots of coffee a day. The big thing for these patients is motor-type problems. If they're coming in with a lot of twitches, jerks and stuff like that we always ask first about stimulants, caffeine, nicotine, medicines that have caffeine in them, things like that." So my mother's nicotine-gum habit, while unusual, fit into the general pattern of stimulant abuse that he'd seen before.

These patients, he says, often have withdrawal problems. They're not getting the stimulant at night when they're sleeping but their body is really used to it, so they're at risk to develop things like seizures, tremors, twitches. When these seizure-type activities don't show up on EEG-type tests, Bell suspects stimulants.

In Mom's particular case, an entire battery of earlier tests failed to find anything beyond the nicotine addiction so finally Bell began to settle on Alzheimer's as the probable cause for her disorientation and her confusion. For Dad, this was news so unwelcome that, at first, he refused to believe it. It must have seemed science-fictional, a kind of horrible alternative universe he'd fallen into. After all, in the world as he'd known it, Bell notes, "He was busy trying to deal with his own troubles, and she had been trying to deal with his troubles, too, so much so that no one was dealing with what was going on with her."

I smiled to hear that from Bell. During the most trying of these times Dad had been pleased when I'd noticed the tremors in his hand. He'd wondered aloud if he, too, shouldn't be seeing that neurologist his wife was seeing.

Bell suspected Parkinson's immediately with Dad and the tests confirmed it. The initial diagnosis, the tests, the confirmation of Parkinson's: all of this took multiple visits to the doctor, which Dad enjoyed, any outing being a good outing in his constricted life.

The prescription was for carbidopa/levidopa, which, Bell explained, replaces the missing dopamine. "In the classic Parkinson's, patients just don't have as many cells that are producing dopamine, so you replace the dopamine directly. The patient takes it in a pill form and it gets broken down in the stomach, gets into the bloodstream, crosses the blood-brain barrier and it's direct."

The drug generally works for about ten years before it becomes less and less effective, Bell told me, but in cases like Dad's the ten-year limit is unlikely to matter and so a physician would, as Bell did, readily prescribe the carbidopa/levidopa.

Bell is enough of a baseball fan (and a Cardinal fan, at that) to recognize and appreciate Dad's connection to the game. For a man who'd been the manager of some very good minor-league baseball teams, and who'd spent a lifetime in a career that required physical grace and strength and strong leadership, the final months had to be terribly difficult.

"That was a big change for him, to be in a position where he couldn't do things, and couldn't get things done," he said. And then, sounding a lot like Grace Lebow, he added, "That's why it's so important [for the children of elderly parents] to try and sit down and try to talk about what's going on and who's going to handle what.

"It's challenging when it's a parent like that. Sometimes it can be a real nightmare. I have a patient who was a judge. She was very strong and now it's just a horrible case. Her daughter cannot communicate with her at all, and so now her daughter calls me every week to step in and tell Mom she can't go on a trip, or can't drive. And we really can't do that, legally, anymore. It's a problem that really requires the kids sitting down with the parent and communicating and driving it home over and over again and finally they'll accept it. They may fight tooth and nail, but it's a necessary role reversal, and there's nothing harder. I had one kid literally tell me that, saying 'I can't do that.' Well, you have to. You simply have to. That's always the most challenging for me, in fact, is when the family wants me to take over. I have to sit down and tell them I can't take over, you have to take over. I had to do that with my own dad, I had to take over. I had to get him off alcohol, get him off cigarettes, make sure he took his meds. A smoker, he died of lung cancer at age 50. I would never have guessed that I'd be able to do that, but you just do it."

I thought of Dad as Bell talked. I thought of the ballplayer, the manager, trapped in a situation where everyone seemed to have let him down.

149

He wanted me to love him best and pay attention to him the most. He wanted this so dearly that he sometimes pitted my love for him against my love for my son. It was a tragic way to live the last months of his life.

But then, a few days later, I talked again briefly with Joe Springle and he said this to me: "You know, you have to choose to remember it otherwise. Over time, you come to realize that that part of their life is only a small part of a long life. When it happens, it's fresh and dominant and you play it over and over again in your mind. But time does allow that lifespan perspective to be there for you.

"The important thing is to recognize that the terrible last days are only that; the terrible last days."

Which is true. And today, as I write, I'm working on that recognition and I'm thinking that maybe, at last, I'm getting there. But it sure hasn't come easy.

16

Bridges: May 2002

I was on my way to work on a sunny Florida morning in May.

Mother's Day, the day before, had been horrible; Dad's telephoned demands had been incessant and angry, at least a dozen calls, each one ratcheting up the venom from the one before. He wanted things. And Now! He didn't care that it was Mother's Day and I was spending it with wife and family. He didn't care that I planned on playing basketball with my Down syndrome son and kicking the soccer ball around with my daughter and pampering my hard-working wife. He didn't care: he wanted things. And Now!

My patience with him was long gone. My struggles with the caregiving role had brought me little but turmoil and disappointment at every turn for most of the previous year and I'd learned to expect anger and demands and disappointment and guilt from him and from Mom and from myself. But yesterday had been at a whole new level and that was especially depressing. If this was a new, darker level I was falling to, it was one I didn't think I could handle.

I'm normally a pretty cheery guy and often too optimistic for my own good, but the months of dealing with Dad and Mom and their individual and collective troubles had changed me. Physically, my hair was turning gray at an amazing rate and I'm as self-conscious about my fading youth as any baby-boomer so this dismayed me. My face felt, and looked, haggard. I felt tired all day long. My sleep was poor as I tossed and turned. I was growing old, and fast, right before my very eyes in the morning mirror each day.

Caregiver stress, I was discovering, has physical as well as mental and emotional costs.*

I'd always prided myself on staying in pretty good shape and I'd spent my life enjoying some daily exercise, but there was no time for that these days: no more jogs on the beach or long bike rides up and down the alleyways and roads of Pass-a-Grille, Florida. Instead, each day brought a too-long list of challenges and commitments ranging from the serious (doctor's appointments) to the frivolous (bacon cheeseburgers, and get one here Now). It seemed the more I did for my father the more demanding he became and so I came to feel I was in some sort of hamster wheel where I ran harder and harder and got nowhere. He was insatiable.

The Mother's Day insanity had capped a bad stretch of escalating demands. Two weeks before Dad had taken a turn for the worse, a sudden infection nearly claiming him. Quick and effective work in the emergency room at nearby Pasadena Community Hospital had saved his life and, chastened by the experience, for a few days he'd been to me the father he was to my brothers: a charming, thoughtful guy who wanted to talk about sports and the grandchildren and the weather and how great it was to be alive. But the respite was a brief one. As soon as his strength returned the truculence and the demands came back with it. I should have done something about it. I should have sought help. But I didn't know how, or know whom to talk to. I felt isolated, I felt tired. I felt used up and empty.

On that first day of Dad's crisis I'd received a worried phone call from the assisted-living facility, telling me that Dad had a fever that had suddenly spiked to a deadly 104 and that he was in an ambulance on the way to the hospital. In twenty minutes I was in the ER with him, where I stayed there for several long hours as his fever raged and we thought we'd lost him. Finally he rallied and, a few hours later, when he seemed to be stable and on the mend, I'd returned home to send this e-mail to my brothers and sisters.

From: Rick Wilber
Sent: April 27, 2002
To: Update list
Subject: update 04/27/02

Hello, all. Here's the update, in brief. I'll post something longer later, because it's been a very interesting day.

*Science News Online, *Week of July 5, 2003; Vol. 164, No. 1.*

Skip's fever is down to 99.9 and dropping, so the antibiotics are kicking in nicely. He's asleep in Room 314 in Palms of Pasadena. You can call the room directly tomorrow. I'll get the number. It was a massive UTI (urinary tract infection). No infection in the lungs.

The bad news: when X-raying the lungs they found very bad news, indeed. The doctor pulled me aside, showed me the shadows and said it looks like lung cancer to him, and spreading widely. He also thought the heart looked like congestive heart failure (despite the OK EKG for Skip). They'll do more tests tomorrow and let us know. If it is what they think, it's weeks or months [he has left], not years.

The same doc, incredibly, has a baseball from St. Pete in 1947, signed by all the Cardinals. He's bringing it in tomorrow. Imagine the circular harmonies there, that this is the doc working on Skip, who signed that ball in the same town fifty-five years ago. Weird Twilight Zone stuff. Skip smiled.

We'll know more tomorrow about the lung cancer and the heart. And the infection. I didn't get into how He wanted the docs and nurses to pay special attention to Him. He kept raising that right arm. I kept asking what he wanted, that he couldn't just make me guess. He just stared at me and kept it raised. I kept telling him there were other sick people, it's an emergency room. Oh, yeah, he said, finally, dropping the arm.

But when the fever hit 104 and he was shaking and they were all really worried around him, I sure told him I loved him.

Over the next couple of weeks Dad rallied, getting stronger as the infection waned. He returned to the assisted-living facility's nursing-home unit where the daily care helped him recover. The recovery, though, had a downside, as my e-mails to my siblings made clear. By this time in many of the e-mails I'd taken to routinely capitalizing the pronouns "He" or "His" or "Him," when they referred to Dad, because he certainly seemed to me to think of Himself that way. Finally, came Mother's Day and the single most depressing day I'd ever been through.

From: Rick Wilber
Sent: May 12, 2002
To: Update list
Subject: update 04/12/02

Hi, all.

The downside of Skip feeling better is that He's calling me all the damn time. First, at 8 A.M., He wants to know when I'm picking Him up today to take Him to the doctor (He's happy about that—He's always happy to go the doctor, I suppose because the focus of that trip is where it belongs, on Him, and it—is—a kind of outing in what is, sadly, an otherwise very constricted life). I told Him it's Sunday, and that the doc is tomorrow, and that I'm not taking Him anyway, Care Ride is and I'll meet Him there. Oh, yeah, He says, and adds Happy Mother's Day. We hang up. I'm worried, frankly, about how poorly he's remembering all the details lately. I've told him all this at least half-a-dozen times.

Then He called an hour later wanting to know about the [sale of the] house. I don't know, I told Him, which was a wholly unsatisfactory answer, He made very clear to me.

Then He called twenty minutes ago, wanting to know where Taffy was. Well, I couldn't answer that, but said I'd try and find out. We'll go by and see her later.

So I expect calls all day and on into the healthier future. I'd sure appreciate it if you all would take the heat off a little bit by calling Him and telling Him how great He is. I'd just quit answering the phone and that would solve it, but we have some soccer organizing going on for a tournament and I'm in charge and so I—have—to answer the phone.

I know, I know, this is something he can do and it's a welcome sense of empowerment for him and all that crap, but I need a break.

A reminder: His number is: (727) 812-3975.

At least two of them called him, but it didn't help. A couple of hours later I sent this e-mail:

From: Rick Wilber
Sent: May 12, 2002
To: Update list
Subject: update 05/12/02

Just so you can get a feel for this, I'm going to send an e-mail after every Skip phone call. Just had #4.

He was in full rampage. They found her, He said, on the fourth floor. He said He gave them Hell. I explained the fourth floor is where the room is for people like Taffy to do things; macramé, TV, books and magazines, painting, etc. etc. That room on the third floor isn't ready yet.

"Well, if that's not ready, what the hell are you doing putting her there. Leave her up on the eleventh floor" [where their apartment had been in better days].

I said I didn't want to be responsible for her taking a taxi to San Antonio.

He got angry.

I got angry.

He hung up.

Call him. Today. Soon.

The downhill spiral continued, and I sent this e-mail a few hours later.

From: Rick Wilber
Sent: May 12, 2002

To: Update list
Subject: update 05/12/02

So, my grand plan hasn't worked. You've been calling him and been nice to him and he's been nice to you and all it did was earn me three more phone calls. He commands my presence and Now! For no particular reason.

I reminded him that on Sunday I play basketball with Rich and spend time with Rich and hang out with Rich and nothing ever goddamn gets in the way of it, even Lord Wilber's commands.

Well, I didn't phrase it quite that way, but I was firm. Which pissed him off. Good. My feeling is that I see him every other fucking day, so Sundays, goddamn it, I spend with Rich and I absolutely fucking refuse to feel guilty about that no matter how much of that he tries to lay on me. No fucking thanks. I'll fucking get to him when I fucking get to him. Jesus Christ.

So. Let's see. That's five times I used "fucking." And two "goddamns." Thanks, all, for putting up with that. I feel better.

Now I'm going to go hang out some more with Rich, who just beat me 15–11.

Del, He commandeth me to call you. Based on the way he said it, I'd prefer it if you call me because I just absolutely can't do anything he commands of me in that fashion. It's too humiliating.

Jesus. What a day.

It went on. I asked him to quit calling but he was in full fury, feeling better after beating back that urinary tract infection and raring to go. Within a couple of hours I sent along this note.

From: Rick Wilber
Sent: May 12, 2002
To: Update list
Subject: update 05/12/02

He called me to tell me that Cindy called and then commandeth me to call Mary.

I said no. Which pissed him off. We argued some more. I told him I thought I'd done my work for today, sending out e-mails and asking you all to call and sure enough you'd called and wasn't that great?

Well, yeah, it's great, but he wants Mary to call. Now! And wants me to make that happen.

I refused.

Finally, by later afternoon, I'd had it and got into the car to go see him, an act which was, I knew even as I did it, teaching the wrong lessons: gripe and complain and demand and, sure enough, #2 son (as he called me) will come by and pay attention. But I felt I had no choice. After that, I sent along this note.

From: Rick Wilber
Sent: May 12, 2002
To: Update list
Subject: update 05/12/02

I went by to see Skip and have it out with him. When I walked in he reached out to take my hand and say he was sorry. Mary had just talked him with on the phone and Mary, whatever you said to him, it worked.

Still, I told him this was way, way out of line. Two phone calls a day from now on, I said, and no more. I have a family. I have to write and teach. In short, I have a life and I can't spend all my minutes answering the phone from him and doing his bidding.

He said he was sorry and that he understood. He said the problem was the phone was right there and it was easy to call me even though he knew it was wrong because it felt like he was doing something. Surprisingly introspective for Skip, I thought.

Dinner came while I was there. French onion soup, chicken salad sandwich with potato salad on the side, juice and soda to drink. Looked pretty good. He started chowing and I left to find Taffy.

I'd bought her a card (and signed it: "From all your children. We love you") and a little plaster St. Pete Beach dolphin thing. Also seven packages of Dentyne (three packs in each package).

I found her with an aide on the way back to her room, so I took her there. Two different things of flowers were in there, one from Bob and other from ... the card was ripped. Del? Not sure. Anyway, they looked great.

She was totally out of it and confused. She even forgot that she chewed gum!!!! Imagine that. She wanted to know why I'd brought that. Wow.

But she was glad to hear that she lived in Florida.

She was also very glad to hear that Skip wasn't in her room. I don't know what we're going to do about that if he continues to make progress. She's quite happy without him and says she doesn't want him back, for whatever her reasons.

Anyway, though totally addled she was very, very pleasant and happy.

Quite a day.

"Quite a day" doesn't begin to convey the stress. I felt like I'd been hit by an emotional truck: and that was after the concern over his health as he fought with the urinary tract infection. I'd been there for him every step of the way during that struggle, starting with standing next to him in the emergency room holding his hand as they started the antibiotic drip that saved his life. I'd been there for him every day for the long months before that, too, and somehow this was what I was getting in return. He was playing me like a fiddle, or moving me around in his lineup like a manager perhaps, and I was feeling pretty damn sorry for myself.

Now it was the next morning at seven A.M. and I was driving to work. It's a long commute, nearly an hour, from our beach town in St. Petersburg all the way across the bay to Tampa and then up the interstate to the northeast side of the metro area and the University of South Florida's Tampa campus, where I teach. Normally I listen to the car radio while I drive, trying to catch the traffic report before I reach a critical juncture or two where I can slip off the highway and take the back roads if there's a jam.

But this morning's jam had nothing to do with traffic, and back roads weren't the answer. Instead, as I drove along, forgetting to sip from my coffee cup, forgetting to turn on the radio, I thought through how things had gone for the past year and how I just seemed to be diving to deeper and darker depths. I'd come to realize that I really couldn't handle it, any of it: the incessant demands, the constant badgering, the phone calls, the guilt. There was never a break, there was never time to recover. My father was just awful and he was constant in that awfulness and there didn't seem to be anything I could do about it and I didn't see an end to it anytime soon. He'd rallied again from this latest bout of terrible health and in doing that he'd gone from a brief two weeks of good behavior back to the bad old habits that I couldn't seem to get away from.

Driving past the Thirty-eighth Street exit I slid over into the fast lane on Interstate 275. St. Petersburg drivers are provably dangerous and I didn't often get into this lane, where someone was likely to tailgate you at seventy miles per hour even when there was a line of cars in front of you. People died on this interstate way too often. It was a form of deadly combat just getting to work in the morning and so I usually tried to stick in the middle lanes, where the insanity was marginally less and one might live a little longer.

But I wasn't all that concerned with living longer right at the moment, I thought. And in having that thought I realized I was contemplating suicide. This was a novel concept for me; I'd never felt the slightest impulse to take my own life. Hell, I'm a science-fiction writer — or was before I took over caring for Dad and watched my writing time and my career disappear — and I'd spent my life wanting to live forever and inventing science-fictional ways to do just that. I'd been proud to say to myself at my annual self-indulgent introspective look back at the end of each year that every year as far back as I could recall had offered me enough new delights to make it better than the year before.

But now Dad had straightened me out on my Pollyanna problem. It had taken me until I was in my fifties, but I'd discovered that Life Is Not Like That. Life doesn't get better and better. Life can really suck, in fact, and this year had been hell, with more of it, apparently, to come. Dad might, in fact, live on for a while. The thought of that appalled me. What if he did live for another year? Another two years? Five? I wouldn't survive it. My god, I thought, I wished he would just die and be done with it.

Yesterday had been the worst day of them all and if this was the start of some new level of rotten behavior I was really and truly in for it. All those phone calls, all those demands. I wanted very much to continue to feel sorry for the guy, whose life was lonely and tightly boxed. But the tone of his voice, the insistent and incessant demands, the constant need for attention: a year of this had worn me down. I really couldn't take it anymore. I had to accept defeat. I had to Do Something. I wanted this to end, and there was only one way that could happen. Thing was, you're not supposed to want your father to die, and just having the thought brought me new waves of guilt. I couldn't do enough for him and all my attempts to rein him in had failed. I couldn't hold myself together while trying to meet his demands. I couldn't even begin to meet my job commitments, my family commitments and his needs, all at the same time.

It was all pretty damn terrible, as I thought on it. And then, ahead, I saw I was coming up on the exit for Fifty-Fourth Street. The street crosses the interstate on a large overpass. The middle abutments of that overpass were coming up ahead, just to my left. I could, I thought, just turn the steering wheel to the left and then I'd hit that abutment and that would end a lot of things. There'd be no more phone calls, no more demands, no more anger, no more of his disappointment when I couldn't respond quickly enough.

There it was, coming up now on the long, gentle downhill slide of the road. I was going seventy miles per hour but there seemed to be a lot of time to think about it, mulling over the implications of this simple action. There was me, the car, the concrete and that, I thought, would be that. Nothing would get better, to be sure, but nothing would get worse, and that was what mattered to me at that moment; stopping the slide.

Then it occurred to me in that strange and leisurely moment that my Down syndrome son needed me and he is the best person I know in any of several ways. And my daughter, bright and athletic and beautiful: she needed me, too. And my wife, the great-looking blonde who turned out to be a whole lot smarter than me and wound up with a doctorate in finance, doing math I can't begin to understand: she needed me, too. These people mattered dearly to me, and they still seemed to love me despite all the zaniness of the past months and what it had done to my usual temperament. It would be foolish, downright selfish and stupid, to let the old man get in the way of the love I had with them.

So I steered right instead of left. And went to campus. And taught my classes. And, over time, wrote this book.

17

Memorabilia

A BASEBALL FROM 1950 SITS next to the keyboard in my office at home. The ball is autographed by Dick Sisler, Blix Donnelly, Richie Ashburn (who signs it Rich), Andy Seminick, Del Ennis, Ken Heintzelman, Eddie Waitkus, Bill Nicholson, Jim Konstanty, Bubba Church (who signs it Bub), and Robin Roberts.

That's the core of the 1950 Philadelphia Phillies: the Whiz Kids. Manager Eddie Sawyer and coaches Benny Bengough and Cy Perkins have autographed it, as well.

The portion of the ball where the seams narrow has a script "Phillies 1950" over a colored-in blue background. Where the seams widen there is a cartooned back wall of Ebbets Field and a pennant saying "Champs." In the opposite wide portion of the seams is a top view of the park with a dotted line showing the route of Sisler's home-run into the left-field seats that won the game, and the pennant, for the Phillies, on the final game of the season.

My father cartooned that ball, got the players to sign it, then shellacked the ball to preserve it, as he did with hundreds of such historic moments in baseball from the late 1930s into the 1970s, preserving them on that most appropriate canvas, each ball a slice of baseball history marked by a cute cartoon, a few cryptic comments, a line-score, and player autographs.

Most of the balls Dad simply gave away. Cartooning and painting baseballs was a hobby for him, something with which to while away the time on long train-rides or in the off-season. But some of the baseballs stuck around, and my brothers and sisters and I still have a few dozen packed away in various boxes and crates. With the painted balls that are in my possession I can pretty much follow the course of Dad's career.

There is, for instance, a ball from 1938, Dad's first year in Class D ball in Findlay, Ohio. The ball lists the manager, Grover A. Hartley, and some of the players: Wilber, Klann, Rami, Stewie (a nickname, perhaps?), Berger, Harris, McKenna, Simons, Roth, Reninger, May, Cook, Prussing, and Kieber. Then there's one from 1939 that shows a pennant with "Champs" written on it for Findlay's winning the Ohio State League title that year. That ball too, lists the players; Cindric, Stephenson, Todhunger, Simons, Cannon, Wilber, Ruley, Fletcher, May, Roth, Brown, Smith, Flynn, Prussing and Horvath. Another ball does the same for the team he played for in 1940, the Springfield, Missouri, Cardinals. That ball lists Mabrey, Vallina, Powers, Smith, Koval, Asbury, Zera, Wilber, Molina, Bush, Bennington, Hopkins, Donnelly, Povichs, Kiepers, and player/manager George Silvey.

For 1941 there's a ball that does the same for Columbus, Georgia, where Dad lists Beal, Streza, Stanton, Fowler, Lucas, Filo, Danaher, Knoblauch, Wilber, Filter, Sisler, Jefferson, Smith, Creel, Beers, Ferens, Green, and manager Clay Hooper.

From the post-war years there's a painted ball from 1947 that's labeled "Del Wilber's Record Ball" and shows his record for the season, playing in fifty-two games and hitting .237. It also shows the record for the other two Cardinal catchers that year, Joe Garagiola (seventy-seven games and .267) and Del Rice (ninety-seven games caught and a .218 average). This ball lists the stats for all the Cardinals, shows their final place in the National-League standings (second, to Brooklyn) and even gives the attendance for the Cardinals at home and away (1,247,931 at home, a record; and 1,513,893 on the road).

A ball from 1948 notes that on Thursday night, August 26th (just nine days before I was born), Dad was the official star of the game with three runs-batted-in on three hits.

From 1949, when Dad was player/manager in the Texas League, there are a couple of balls that celebrate his home runs for the Houston Buffs. One ball describes his first home run of the season, off Blankenship of Beaumont on May 27th, and adds that the homer won him "a new suit and a new watch." Another notes a July 1st grand-slam home run off Shreveport's Jack Krause in the tenth inning.

From Dad's year in Rochester, New York, in 1950 there's a ball, the lacquer on it browned with age, that shows him in a hitting pose and a catching pose and lets me know that he wore number twenty-three that year.

From the next year, Dad's best single season when he played well for the Phillies, I have a guest ball, cartooned and signed by the artist: Geo. H. Sosnak. The ball celebrates Dad's memorable three-homer game that still resonates for all of us in his family despite its surprising commonality.

Other balls from the 1950s include one from his coaching years with the White Sox, cartooned especially for Dad's father-in-law, Posey Archibald Bennett of San Antonio, Texas. The cartoon shows a figure of a guard saying "You don't need a pass at this gate, P.A." The ball lists the manager and coaches for that White Sox team: Marty Marion, Ray Berres, Don Gutteridge, George Myatt and Del Wilber. It also lists the players from that excellent White Sox team which included the likes of Nellie Fox, Minnie Minoso, Larry Doby, Billy Pierce, Luis Aparicio and others.

Other balls provide snapshots of Dad's career as a minor-league manager, where he enjoyed considerable success. The balls, happily, are autographed and include three from the American Association all-star games of 1960 and 1971 and '72. These balls and some others from his playing and coaching days include autographs from many of the game's greatest names, the 1960 all-star game ball, for instance, signed by Carl Yastrzemski, Jim Kaat, Lee Maye, Bill Adair, Ray Jablonski and others. The 1972 all-star ball is signed by Jim Bibby, Ken Reitz, Manny Trillo, Lance Coleman, and others. Another, undated but earlier ball, is signed by Walker Cooper, Johnny Mize, Leo Durocher, Andyk Pafko, Richie Ashburn, Pee Wee Reese, Enos Slaughter and others.

One ball, worn enough that it looks as if it saw play before being autographed, is signed by Mike Hargrove, Tom Grieve, Len Randle, Billy Martin, Jeff Burroughs, Jim Bibby, David Clyde, Fergie Jenkins, Toby Harrah and others. I'd like to think this ball saw an inning of action in the one major-league game that Dad managed, and won.

Yet another ball must have come from a Pacific Coast League game, perhaps an exhibition in Hollywood: it's a Pacific Coast League ball signed by Shecky Green, Brian Keith, Rob Reiner, and Ernest Borgnine, among others.

When Dad died he left behind a wealth of things to remember him by. In a haphazard sharing of the memorabilia of his life we divided up the cartooned baseballs and parceled out other things, as well. I wound up with a lot of newspaper and magazine clips and a wealth of photographs of family and friends, almost always centered on baseball. I also have some personal correspondence, love letters from Dad to Mom as he was courting her during the war. They are touching and earnest and obviously they worked.

I also have a small plaque that says "Del Wilbur [*sic*]. 'One in a Million' and 'Spokane's Favorite Manager, 1974.'" The Indians won the pennant that year, so the plaque is well-earned, if misspelled. And then there's a championship ring from the previous year, that reads "Spokane Indians" along the sides and PCL Champions across the top. There's a watch from the 1971 American Association All-Star game, and another watch from 1996 that reads "50th Anniversary 1946 World Champions" around the outside of the face and "St. Louis Cardinals" in the middle. Dad played briefly for that team before heading to the minors for the rest of the season, but half a century later the Cardinals included him in the anniversary celebration.

There's more: a White Sox cufflink, a tiny brass baseball bat and ball that reads "Rochester Red Wings 1950," and, best of all, a small octagonal medal that reads "Frank G. Mixter Medal" on the front side and "1937, Scholarship and Athletic Efficiency, Lincoln Park High School" across the back.

"Efficiency?" I'm not sure what that means and can only assume that in high-school he was a good student as well as a good athlete, or at least an efficient one.

He was a generous father, in his own way. He gave us, after all, Fenway and Shibe and Sportsman's and Comiskey and all those minor-league parks, as well.

He gave us, too—or at least some of us—his athletic grace. Both of my brothers played college and professional baseball and both of my sisters were good athletes, too, though in those pre–Title IX days they didn't get much of a chance to prove it.

I, meanwhile, mostly read books, perhaps because they didn't curve. I made the high-school football and baseball teams and got a few varsity letters. I even got a football scholarship to the University of Minnesota (with Dad's help, I suspect: he could be very persuasive when it came to promoting the athletic careers of his sons). There I discovered that college football demanded more of me than I had to give. By the time I was halfway through college I'd been forced to realize that it was time to grow up and find real things to do, things that weren't necessarily tied so firmly to sports. Eventually, I started to write and teach, which felt productive to me if not particularly heroic and certainly not larger than life. Bookish or not, though, I was still a ballplayer's son, still part of baseball's family. It was, by god, a hell of a way to grow up. And so I owed him.

It was a difficult year, watching him slowly go and trying as best I could to help him and Mom deal with their decline. But we had a few good innings here and there in this otherwise dismal time. The Parkinson's had him trembling badly, but the carbidopa/levidopa he took calmed the tremors down well enough that he could again sign autographs. I helped him with that, opening the mail, bringing him the three-by-five cards that fans wanted autographed, taking a bit of dictation from him now and again to write a brief response when a fan had a question about what it was like to catch Robin Roberts or stand at the plate against Warren Spahn or sit in the dugout next to Ted Williams.

And the cataract surgery he went through was a success, the clouded lenses of his eyes replaced by new implants so he could return to watching baseball on ESPN as often as he wanted. Even the deadly prostate cancer responded, for a time, to several different drugs meant to slow its progress. But there was no surgery, there were no wonder drugs, for his attitude, with which I struggled and ultimately lost, making worse, I think, a terribly difficult time for a terribly difficult man.

Of course he wasn't that way with everyone, or with anyone, really, except me; not so much of because of who I am, I learned later, but because of what I did, serving as his caregiver. In all but his very darkest days he remained friendly and gregarious toward his other sons, for instance, and toward his grandchildren. Toward his daughters he showed a different face, a less happy one, and to me he was often obstreperous and difficult. But I've learned that this is often how the caregiver is viewed by the very people he or she is helping.

His two other sons benefited from visiting less often and from the history he'd shared with them. He'd been, after all, a great father to his youngest son, who'd been just the right age to be a batboy on several minor-league teams that Dad managed in the 1970s. And Dad had always been attentive and proud of his first-born son, who repaid that love and attention with academic and athletic success throughout his school years, followed by a few years of solid minor-league play and then a hugely successful career in the business of sports.

I think I'd always wanted some small part of the love and attention those two sons had received, and bringing Dad and Mom to St. Petersburg was my chance. Perhaps that was selfish of me. Perhaps I expected too much. But what I found instead of love in that trying time was profoundly hard work, as so many men and women—the adult children of elderly parents—do when they take on the caregiver role.

I am a journalism professor, a writer and a family man: it's a good and busy life. But during my time as caregiver I came to realize that meeting my parents' needs meant changes—major changes—had to be made in my life. Certain things just wouldn't get done. My own family, of course, came first, but after that everything was open for discussion.

I still taught my regular course load, but not nearly as well as I'd have liked. In the writing courses, in particular, the students, frankly, didn't get the editing attention they deserved. In a few instances, mostly with graduate students, I simply had to explain the demands on my time at home and apologize for the slowness and thinness of my critiques. Most of the students seemed understanding; but a few complained and I couldn't blame them.

On the writing side, I had one co-authored journalism textbook about ready to turn in to the publisher, so I struggled along with that, relying more and more on my co-author as the stresses grew at home. And I had a novel under contract and I had to finish it. The novel meant a lot to me, so I remained determined to work on it, as well, though the work went poorly and the final version wasn't all that I'd hoped it would be.

Everything else pretty much took a distant back seat. That feature-writing textbook under contract? Sorry. The second edition of the magazine-writing textbook? The short stories that I love to write? The poetry? The follow-up novels, two of which were half-done? Sorry, sorry, sorry, sorry, sorry.

These were my parents and they now lived in my town. I realized they weren't going to be as independent as we grown children had thought or hoped, and so it fell upon me to help. (It's all about geography, one brother told me when I complained about the workload.) In the midst of this stressful confusion I came to realize that a large part of the problem was how my father viewed the world. His expectations weren't those of more ordinary

165

men, like, say, doctors or lawyers or firefighters or policemen or plumbers or presidents of great corporations. He thought himself above all that. He expected better treatment. He had, after all, played in the big leagues. He expected attention: a lot of attention (and prompt attention, at that).

For instance, in the ophthalmologist's office during the long string of pre-op and post-op visits for his cataract surgeries, he would, without fail, raise that right arm up high in a call for attention when the doctor came within view, sometimes saying "Hey!" and sometimes staying quiet. It was a sort of baseball loyalty test, and to pass it the doctor had to notice Dad and talk to him, saying something baseball, and promising to see him soon. Then, his needs met for the moment, Dad would wait, impatiently, for the office visit. If another ten minutes went by (I actually timed this on several occasions) he would start griping at me every minute or so as if I could, or should, do something about the wait.

For a backup catcher from a half-century before, I came to think, he sure had an interesting view of his own importance. Somehow he'd come to the conclusion that hitting three home runs in one game in 1951 conferred on him a lifetime exemption from the common rules of polite behavior that governed other, lesser, men. There should be no standing in line, no waiting, for Del Wilber, major-leaguer.

And here's the thing that amazed me the most: Those other, lesser men seemed to agree with him. In the office of the oncologist, the urologist, the ophthalmologist, the neurologist, the primary-care doctor, the optometrist— everywhere, it was the same: Dad would admit, when prodded, that he'd been a ballplayer in that hazy, golden past of baseball. Yes, he'd known and played with Ted Williams and Joe Garagiola and Robin Roberts and Stan the Man and on and on.

Always, someone else in the waiting room had been to a game at Ebbets or Shibe or Fenway or Yankee Stadium or any of the other hallowed halls of those days, and yes, they thought maybe they remembered seeing him play. Hadn't he hit a pinch-hit home run in Boston to send the game into extra innings in 1954? Sure he had, and could describe the sequence of pitches. Wasn't he the player who'd been paid a bonus to room with Jimmy Piersall? Sure he was, and he hadn't minded it, he'd always been one to get along with everyone and anyone (hearing that one for the first time, I rolled my eyes and sighed).

Baseball's collective memory, I came to realize, is powerfully evocative and astoundingly complete, one story leading into the next until, finally, autographs signed, blood drawn, several stories told, blood pressure taken and shot of Lupron given, we'd head back to his apartment in the assisted-living facility.

There were any number of times during Dad's final year when I was angry and hurt by his behavior. At first, I simply accepted this, thinking it a temporary reaction to the move and his wife's decline. Later, I started to open up and tell him I was bothered. Each time, he would profess to be sorry, he would say he understood and things would, briefly, get better. But the center never held and within a day or two Dad would go right back into full command mode, calling me on the phone to demand I bring him a Wendy's bacon cheeseburger, and Now. It was a frustrating, difficult time, so much so that I often simply unplugged the phone to win an evening's respite.

But then there were times when I'd sit next to him and he'd start telling about the game as it was and we'd both smile as the stories spun out—some of them ones I'd heard before, others brand new, conjured up from the days of Stan the Man and the Splinter and the Whiz Kids and the Go-Go Sox. The one he loved best to relate was of the time he'd been, for one golden day, larger than life. He told it to me again just a few weeks before he died:

On August 27 of 1951, Cincinnati's Ken Raffensberger was pitching when Del Wilber—the back-up catcher to Andy Seminick, but starting the second game of the double-header—came to the plate in the bottom of the third.

Raffensberger's first pitch was, Dad recalled, a sinker down low for ball one. The second pitch was a "big, sloppy curve, over the plate" for strike one. The third pitch was a slider that hung up and over the plate. Dad took it deep into left, into the upper deck of Shibe Park for a one-run Phillies lead in the bottom of the third.

Raffensberger pitched a fine game as the innings passed, except for that one mistake to Del Wilber. A few innings later Dad came up again. The first pitch was a sinker, low, for ball one. The second pitch was another sloppy curve for strike one. Dad recognized the pattern and, he told me in some detail fifty years later, he thought it was worth guessing at the next pitch. Sure enough, in came the slider and Dad rode it out of the park down the left-field line. Home run number two.

The next time he came up, in the bottom of the eighth, the score was still two-to-nothing on his two homers. Dad figured Raffensberger had to deck him, and was ready for it. Instead, in came that sinker, low, for ball one. Then the sloppy curve for strike one, followed, fat as a melon now given the day's history, that slider. Dad swung, and in connecting became the only player to hit three home runs to score all three runs in a 3–0 game. It was the third pitch each time, too, and in every third inning.

Was that game worth all the difficulties in these final years? Hundreds of players have hit three home runs in a game and Dad's three-homer day is remembered today only for its trivia merit, the fact that all three runs in a three-run game were scored by one player hitting it out three times. Were the moments of those home runs and the other few he hit in eight years of play sufficient to explain his behavior? Was being a ballplayer enough to explain his need for attention, his need to be special?

Sure it was. After all, we all think we're special, we all live in a private world where everything revolves around us and our wants and needs. It's just that most of us, from time to time, face the hard news that our private fantasy is just that. Dad, bless his selfish baseball heart, never had to face that news.

I wanted to get to know my father before he was gone and I did that. It didn't go much the way I'd thought it would, but that's all right, I learned a lot about him and Mom that I hadn't known before. Some of what I learned brought me joy and respect for them. Most of it, to be gentle, didn't. But all of it—better late than never—taught me something about myself, too; something about who I am now and who I'd like to be in thirty years.

I had it out with Dad several times over the course of that year, trying to clear the air and lower the stress. When I went to visit with him at the end of that miserable Mother's Day when he raised the stress levels through the roof, I was surprised by how apologetic he was. His sincerity rattled me, the guilt welling up. Shouldn't I just let him be? Shouldn't I just cater to whatever he wanted in these final months? The combination of anger and guilt held enormous power over me and that, I suppose, is why I considered steering into the abutment on that interstate overpass.

So I tried hard to be the supportive son I knew I should be and, I think, he tried hard, too. Toward the end, we were calm, Dad and I. He was, in fact, downright nice, some sort of late-inning politeness rally going on.

I took a micro-cassette recorder in with me to capture his stories during those final weeks. His smoker's lungs were congested and cancer-ridden, his heart struggling with the strain. When I left for three weeks in July to run my annual summer school in Ireland I knew it might be the last time I'd see him. He was weak, but smiling. I told him I loved him. I squeezed his hand.

He said thanks, which was about as close as he could get, I think, to loving me back.

The last story he told me, the day before I left, was of the time as a White Sox coach when he sneaked into the Comiskey Park scoreboard to steal the catcher's signs. He was cheating and he knew it, but he thought of it, rightly or wrongly, as part of the game. "We had the binoculars off a Japanese battleship," he told me. "Johnny Rigney [a White Sox pitcher in the 1930s and 1940s, by then working in the front office for the Sox] got them when he was at Great Lakes Naval Air Station.

"I'd look down there and see the sign. I used a light bulb in a tomato can. If the light was on it was a curve and if it the light was off it was a fastball."

He laughed. "I called 21 consecutive pitches against Frank Lary with Detroit and he beat us 1–0 in 11 innings so I'm not sure how much it helped."

I listened raptly to this story, not wanting to interrupt, though I had questions about what he thought back then about sportsmanship or rights or wrongs. Instead, I was mesmerized by the sense of it, by the feel of baseball mythology come alive for me listening to my father as he talked about the narrow ladders in the back of the scoreboard and what it was like to climb them, talked about looking out through the opening and peering through the binoculars to see how many fingers the catcher was showing and where he was patting the inside of his thigh to let the pitcher know the placement, talked about setting up the tomato can and plugging in the light. For a few minutes the anger and the worry and the exasperation and the stress of the preceding year — it all washed away and I was back in those days, back when the game was really the national pastime, back when Dad was deeply part of that and so, lucky family, were we.

The game wound its way through us and I can't escape it. Truth is, while I say I hate baseball now, I still play myself when I have the time, doing a decent job at second base in a local over–40 hardball league. If there's a sweeter physical sensation for a man in his fifties than hitting a double into the gap off a forty-year-old pitcher with a good slider, I don't know quite what it is.

Behind that cartooned and shellacked ball on my work-desk is a Christ-

Del Wilber (left), Dick Sisler, Terry Moore, Stan Musial and Red Schoendienst work at a Christmas tree lot in Clayton, Missouri, in December of 1947. Photograph from the *St. Louis Globe-Democrat* Archives of the St. Louis Mercantile Library at the University of Missouri–St. Louis. Reprinted with permission.

mas card I received a couple of years ago from the Baseball Hall of Fame. On the card is a photograph from 1947 that shows, from left to right, Del Wilber, Dick Sisler, Terry Moore, Stan Musial and Red Schoendienst all gathered around a table, ostensibly making Christmas wreaths. My dad is smoking a pipe, smiling with the pipe in his mouth while the other four look at him and grin. They are all wearing Cardinal caps and Cardinal jackets, with the redbird sitting on the bat and each player's number on his left sleeve.

Just a few weeks before he died I asked my dad about that photograph. He remembered the day the picture was taken and told me the story of working at the Christmas tree lot, making a grand total of $96.

He mentioned a conversation he'd had recently with another old Cardinal, Marty Marion. "You know," he said to me "mostly, we talked about how we didn't make any money."

His top salary, he said, was eight-thousand dollars in 1953.

"I was damn lucky," he said. "Marty and I talked about that, about how lucky we were to get to do what we loved for our whole lives."

Yes, I think now, he was lucky. And talented.

"Those were good days," he said.

Yes, I thought, when he said that, they sure were.

18

Life After Baseball

THE WAY DAD TOLD US THE STORY that day at the ophthalmologist's office, it was early March of 1954 when painter Norman Rockwell was in Sarasota, Florida, to do a cover illustration for the *Saturday Evening Post*. The illustration would feature several Red Sox players greeting a young rookie on his first day in the clubhouse. There was a buzz in the Sox's spring-training clubhouse, Dad recalled in delightful detail. Even baseball players knew and liked Rockwell and his famous cover art for the magazine. Most of the players were looking forward to posing for the magazine cover.

But Ted Williams, the Red Sox slugger, was being difficult. Never friendly with the media anyway, Williams was especially unhappy with Rockwell's plan to have him pose at length after the day's workouts were done. Unwilling to waste his time, Ted, petulant, just said no.

But he did offer an alternative. His friend, catcher Del Wilber—who was right-handed but otherwise a suitable body-double at about the same height and weight—could fill in for the hours of posing by the locker that were required, and then Ted could later pause long enough for the painter to capture his face and add it onto the finished body.

Rockwell agreed and so that, said Dad, is how he—or most of him, anyway—came to be on the cover of the *Saturday Evening Post* in a famous illustration called "The Rookie." Dad was a back-up catcher and pinch-hitter that year for the Red Sox, so he was unlikely to get a magazine cover on his own, much less a Norman Rockwell illustration for the *Post*.

172

It was a great story and I was enthralled, hearing it. After all, when I'd first taken on the caregiving duties for Dad and Mom, my expectations had revolved mainly around baseball and storytelling and getting a chance at last to better know the genial old storyteller who'd often been gone in my youth. Somehow I'd missed out on getting to know the man my two brothers worshiped, the man my sister's children revered as a grandfather with a thousand great stories, the grandpa who loved them and cared about them. So here, in the final innings of his life, I was delighted, getting to hear a story I didn't know, which seemed, at the moment, adequate compensation for some other disappointments.

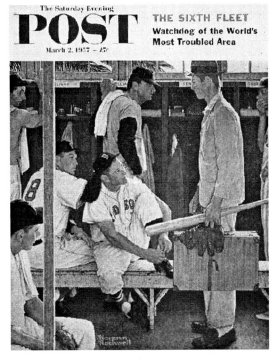

"The Rookie," by Norman Rockwell, was used as the cover art for the *Saturday Evening Post*, March 2, 1957. (Used with permission of Normal Rockwell Family Agency.)

What I'd discovered, unhappily, was one very grumpy and demanding guy. It was a shock, discovering this, since I'd thought of him otherwise. But I came to realize the difference between being a son and being a caregiver is the difference between admiring the great Oz and seeing the sad, elderly man full of bombast behind the curtain. Until I was in charge of his health, his life, his happiness, his sadness, his frustrations, his anger, his occasional moments of joy—until I was in charge of all that I'd thought of my father as garrulous but well-intentioned old ballplayer who was a loving father, a doting grandfather and one heck of a wonderful story-teller. All of that turned out to be true; but there was more to him than that, and it was true, as well, though less happy.

Dad seemed happiest when I brought my children to see him; he was especially warm with my Down syndrome son, the boy who stole his grandpa's heart a long time ago. And he loved hearing a detailed analysis of the latest game from my soccer-playing daughter. But his happiness wasn't their job, it was his. And, I figured, mine; though I wondered often enough when my debt for a happy childhood would be fully paid.

He wasn't like this with my brothers. He kept up the façade with them and remained the charming old ballplayer they knew; full of stories of the glory days of the game and happy, too, to chat about the game today, or their lives in their own sports worlds. They both knew how to play the game and he loved them for that. My older brother visited every month or two, the younger brother a lot less often though he called almost daily.

Once, after a particularly difficult morning when Dad had made a long series of petty telephoned demands of me, I met my older brother in the afternoon at Dad's bedside in the nursing home unit of the assisted-living facility where he and Mom lived. A week before he'd had that infection that nearly killed him. Quick attention and an antibiotic drip had pulled him through and now he was recuperating.

As I walked in, father and son were talking, as always, about baseball. I forget which moment was being remembered, which memory savored: something about Yogi, or Piersall, or Stan the Man. Dad had the bedside telephone in his hand. I took it from him and placed it back in the cradle. In that final, sad year, when so much of his life was physically restricted but his mind was still fine, Dad found the telephone a useful tool—no, a bludgeon—to reclaim the power he'd lost. He called me on the phone every single day, starting early in the morning and ending late at night, griping or demanding or commanding. The old ballplayer needed attention.

On this day, the storytelling with his eldest son had left Dad thirsty. After a year of care, I could tell without needing to hear him say a thing: the wetting of the lips, the dry and shaky voice. I recognized his symptoms and knew he needed a drink. I started to walk around the bed to get over to the small bed stand that was just out of his reach. There was a small bottle of orange Gatorade there. Gatorade was his drink of choice now that the doctor had banned Cokes and it had been ten years since he'd had his daily bottle, or two, of Cabin Still bourbon.

He cleared his throat with that loud, deadly harrumph I'd come to recognize as the precursor to one command or another. "Get me a drink. Now," he was about to say to me. I knew this was coming and I wanted my brother to see it. The father I knew now and the father that both of my brothers knew were two very different people. I wanted my older brother to see this at last.

174

But Dad, consciously or not, threw me a curveball. As I took the first two steps, he cleared his throat, sure enough, but then said this my brother: "Son, could you get me something to drink? Please?"

I was so shocked my jaw dropped open. Please? Did he say please? When did he learn the word? And why did he use it now?

I was furious. I'd spent months putting up with a man so self-centered that he was willing to come between me and my son so he could have a sandwich when he wanted it—which was always Now. And here, out of the blue, he was once again the genial old pro, solicitous of his first son. I almost said something in anger. Perhaps I should have. Instead, I kept it bottled up, as I kept far too much bottled up over that last year of Dad's life. I smiled tightly and let my older brother get the Gatorade and give it to Dad. He couldn't figure out how to get the liquid into Dad's mouth, which took a certain amount of well-practiced aiming, so I stepped in just long enough to direct the stream. I finished, took the bottle from Dad's mouth, and as I walked back to the table Dad said, "Thanks, thanks a lot," to my brother.

This, I now recognize, is part of being a caregiver, moving from being the child to being a parent's loving but stern parent. It is, as I've tried to show, a demanding, confusing role.

Del Wilber was a mediocre big-league ballplayer, to be sure. But it is worth remembering that there were hundreds of thousands of boy in the Depression years who wanted to grow up and be big-leaguers, even mediocre ones, and Dad was one of a talented and lucky few hundred to actually live that dream.

Once he was there he never had the breakthrough he sought for decades. As a player, he enjoyed his one or two decent seasons and another six or seven pretty pedestrian ones. As a manager, he paid his dues for years, waiting patiently in line for his shot at the big-league job that he seemed destined for, and when he got it he held it for just that one game. I suspect that, in the end, this ate at him. He wanted to have done more. Most men might have been satisfied with having lived a good life, provided for a family, seen the children and then grandchildren grow to adulthood safely and mostly happily and with some success. But most men didn't play in the major leagues. Most men didn't hit three home runs in one game in Shibe, or play with Stan the Man or Teddy Ballgame or any of the other great players of the 1940s and 50s. Most men couldn't play The Game.

And that past, unhappily, trapped Dad. He'd spent his life with baseball, and the game had been very good to him in return. But, looking back, he'd been reaching for the brass ring and never quite caught it—or, considering his one major-league win as a manager, he touched the brass ring once, grasped it even, and then saw it pulled away. So, late in life the singular successes, the isolated moments when he rose above the usual to be special, loomed large for him. He wound up embracing being part of the minutiae of baseball, not because he wanted to; but because he had to.

Dad and I struggled to get along in those final months. From my perspective, I was trying to meet both my parents' needs and keep them alive, safe and as happy as possible while still paying attention to my own family and my work. Dad expected a great deal more of me than that and so we argued over my inability to meet his needs. I explained that the point of an assisted-living facility was that he could get all the help he needed whenever he needed it and that I didn't have to be—and couldn't be—available twenty-four hours a day to fetch a bacon cheeseburger from Wendy's or bring him a 12-pack of Diet Coke. I had my own family, I explained, and writers have to write.

He found my explanations insufficient and his disappointment in me was profound, even though I saw him about every day. There was pretty near constant friction and it was stressful. But I always had that one safe haven with him: Dad loved telling stories. No matter how much anger had been tossed back and forth on a given day I could always ask a question about the game and Dad would calm down and start in on some fantastic memory about the Whiz Kids or the Go-Go Sox and just like that, the day would brighten some. I'm sure that whatever abilities I have to find the details that inform and charm and frighten and entertain the reader come from him.

His children, all five of us, loved his baseball stories. We shared them with our own children, shared them with each other, collected memorabilia, wrote books and stories about him and about the game he loved and spent a lifetime playing. But in doing all that, I wonder if we didn't worsen things for Dad in his final year, when the stories were really all that he had to offer. We convinced him that baseball and its glory days were what mattered most to us, and so to him, though we thought it was the other way around. In doing that we were co-dependents in a deep addiction to some better past that we helped him create. He had a narrow life that didn't leave him much room to move around in toward the end and that life was, at least in significant part, our creation as we encouraged him to relate the myths of that hazy baseball past where Rapid Robert and Scooter and Vinegar Bend and dozens of other nicknames played for the love of the game. Worse, while we took pleasure in the stories we'd heard a hundred times before, we got especially excited about the new ones, always upping the ante on poor Dad to conjure up some new amazement.

Dad's story about posing for Norman Rockwell wasn't true. In a routine fact-checking mission for an early draft of this book, I checked with the Norman Rockwell Museum in Stockbridge, Massachusetts, expecting some excitement when the researchers found out that my father had actually done the long, hard work of posing during spring training of 1954 for the illustration that became one of Rockwell's most famous, "The Rookie."

But in doing the fact checking I began to realize that things weren't adding up. The cover illustration in question was for the March 2, 1957, issue of the magazine and Dad's last season with the Sox was 1954. And, the museum explained, by that time in Rockwell's career he used photographs as the basis for his paintings and didn't require lengthy poses from his subjects. In fact, the museum had the list of men who'd posed for photographs for that cover illustration: Sammy White, Jackie Jensen, and Frank Sullivan. It was Sullivan who stood in for Williams. The rookie himself was modeled by Pittsfield High School student Sherman Safford.

Del Wilber wasn't there.

This was a bitter blow for me and for my siblings. For me, the news came one year to the day from the terrible Mother's Day when Dad had called and challenged me to love him more than my wife and my children. I'd been emotionally bruised that day, so shook up by his venom and Mom's continuing confusion and decline that the next morning was the one where I'd considered putting an end to the pain by easing the steering wheel a bit left and finding peace in a large concrete abutment at seventy miles an hour.

And now, a year later, with Dad dead and gone for ten months, I discovered the venom wasn't gone. Now it was my brothers and sisters, most of them, who were furious with me. They didn't like the truth that I'd found and they were outraged at my motives. One brother, the one with a print of that illustration on his office wall, sent me an e-mail full of hurt and anger, saying he couldn't believe I'd done what I'd done and how he'd just rather not know the truth. In the ensuing couple of years his anger seems to have

177

grown and our falling out is complete: I can't communicate with him, though I've tried a few different times.

The tension of that day was so horrific that I felt a sharp, electric jolt in my right shoulder and arm. This was something I'd dealt with for decades, beginning with high-school and then college football, when it had been diagnosed as a pinched nerve. Over the years, at particular times when I'd been stressed and tense, a knot of pain would grow in the area of my neck and the left side of my right shoulder blade. Always, when the stress went away so did the neck and shoulder pain. I learned to live with it.

But on this particular day the pain was extraordinary. The e-mails back and forth, my siblings' hurt and anger and mine in return, their disappointment in me and the way it reminded me of Dad's disappointment in me, their suspicions of just why I dug up this unfortunate truth: all of these things seemed to nurture that knot of pain until I thought I felt it burst and the first electric jab went down my right arm, right to my fingertips. Ouch.

Over the next few days the pain only grew. I'd never experienced that sort of pain before and I didn't know what to do with it. I went to a chiropractor who was a friend who'd earned my trust in his skills by helping me through the inevitable pains of playing baseball in your 50s: he was a teammate and a fine catcher on the over–40 baseball team I'd played on for years. He stretched and manipulated and zapped and probed and it helped, but never for more than a few hours.

A month later, still in considerable pain, I took my daughter with me as we went to a favorite nephew's wedding in a beautiful old chapel in a glen north of San Francisco that wasn't far from George Lucas' Skywalker Ranch. The rehearsal dinner was during a cruise on San Francisco Bay, and we spent time in the Muir Woods, too, communing with the amazing redwoods that rise from that valley. We also spent the day at Stanford University's nature preserve with my sister Cindy, who has helped nurture my daughter's abiding interest in animals and plants. Together, my sister and my daughter spent the day looking at rattlesnakes and lizards and slugs while I sat in pain on the back of a golf cart. My other brothers and sister were there, too, and I did my best to hide my pain—emotional as well as physical—from them. I'm not sure how good a job of that I did.

Ultimately, by August I was in surgery: an anterior discectomy with fusion that a very fine orthopedic surgeon performed on me, going in through the front of the neck to pull out the worn-down disk I'd finally herniated that day when the tensions had risen so high. He removed it and replaced it with donor bone from a cadaver and a titanium plate. When I woke up the pain was gone and the relief from it was so profound that the routine post-operative discomfort felt like nothing. I never took anything more than an ibuprofen for the post-op pain and a couple of days after the surgery I was flying home. I felt better. I felt a lot better, in fact; nearly euphoric with relief. I resolved to never let family stresses get the better of me again and so when siblings issues have arisen since then, all or most of them still revolving around my memories of Dad and my siblings' different versions of those same moments in baseball and personal history, I have tried to just walk away metaphorically. I don't need the pain.

An article on the real truth of that famous painting ran in the *Boston Globe* in May of 2005, almost exactly one year after what I came to think of as The Day of Pain. The article focused on Frank Sullivan, who'd done the actual posing for Rockwell. Ironically, the article pointed out that Sullivan was "blessed with an emotional intelligence that allowed him to flatten his ego when his playing days ended. He worked as a boat jockey taking yachts to and from Florida and labored for peanuts at a marine repair dock in Southwest Harbor, Maine, before skedaddling for Kauai." Why did Sullivan walk away, and why walk so far away? His answer in the article was this: "When you're a jock, people do things for you. It's great as long as you can deliver. The minute you can't, it comes to a screeching halt and reality needs to be addressed. I didn't want to go through that around friends here."

There were more than a few ironies that came to mind as I read that about Sullivan, who not only was the one who'd really posed in place of Williams, but was also the sort of man who could walk from having played for the Red Sox and sought another, different, maybe a better, life. He had a grip on reality that the children of Del Wilber, myself included, didn't seem to have. Why couldn't my brothers and sisters accept that Dad had made up that story, I wondered? Why were they so angry with me?

All but one of my other siblings have been more forgiving of my reporting as time has passed, but mostly they prefer thinking of Dad the old way. Well, me, too; but you can't go back. There are dozens of such stories that are part of our family mythology: Dad using those captured binoculars from a captured Japanese battleship to steal the catcher's signs from his cubbyhole in the Comiskey Park scoreboard. Dad getting paid that extra $50 a day to room with the troubled Jimmy Piersall during the Red Sox years.

Dad advising the Minnesota Twins organization not to mess with Tony Oliva's batting swing early in Oliva's career. Dad helping to found the fall instructional league in Florida in the late 1960s.

Some of these stories are provably true. In his book *Tony O! The Trials and Triumphs of Tony Oliva*, Oliva writes at length about how Dad helped him offensively and defensively in the Florida Instructional League. Oliva wound up being a Gold Glove player and an All-Star. And it was Del Wilber, the book says, who sent the message to Twins' owner, Calvin Griffith, that he should "Fire anyone who tried to change his (Oliva's) batting style." Oliva wound up being one of the game's great hitters. The copy of the book I have is signed by Oliva, and the inscription reads: "To my friend Del Wilber. Thanks for your help in getting me to the big leagues. Best wishes always, Tony Oliva."

Some of the stories, the ones I haven't yet found corroboration for, may not be true, or may be exaggerated. I can't find any verification of Dad's story of rooming with Piersall, for instance. In Piersall's books, *Fear Strikes Out* and the later *The Truth Hurts*, there isn't any mention of Del Wilber, either during Piersall's frightening year of 1952 when he suffered his breakdown, or 1953 when he made his remarkable comeback. Perhaps Dad did room with Piersall in '52, since Jimmy's memories of that year were sketchy at best. Perhaps Dad didn't. This is, I suppose, the risk a great storyteller takes. I've sent a note to the Red Sox to check on the story and I've tried to contact Piersall because I want to know for sure. I am, after all, the second son of Del Wilber, ex–major leaguer, the guy who hit three home runs in one game for the Phillies and won one game as a big-league manager and had more ribbies than hits in 1954 for the Red Sox. To a lot of people, myself included, these things matter. So I plan to keep checking because I know the myths and I want to know the truth. I don't think we have to believe the untruths. Dad lived an interesting life in the game, had several special moments in the sunshine as a player, manager and coach, and helped his wife raise five children and ten grandchildren. That should be enough.

Del Wilber died just thirteen days after Ted Williams' death and the weird drama that swirled around it, when two of Ted's children squabbled over whether or not to cryogenically preserve their father's head in the hopes of later revival, or at least the use of preserved DNA to clone another version of one of the game's greatest hitters. Dad's remains were cremated, and my sister Mary and I, the two who did the hard work of caring for a difficult man in his most difficult days, were the ones who placed the urn into the ground.

I visit the site once a month or so. Just the other day I was there, thinking of Dad and St. Petersburg and spring training and all the stories that came from a life in baseball. I'd brought a baseball with me, a cheap Rawlings I'd bought at a used sporting goods store on my way there. I'd planned to scribble something on it and leave it there in memory of Dad, but I couldn't think of what to write; nothing seemed adequate to the truth. So I just signed it, set it on the plaque, and left it there, surrounded by wide swaths of perfect green grass under a bright Florida sun in that high, blue sky.

19

Post Hoc

I'M AT THE CYPRESS GARDENS ASSISTED-living facility in Sarasota, Florida, with my son, the remarkable Down syndrome guy. About six months after Dad died my sister Mary moved from Orlando to Sarasota and then, with the consent of all her siblings, moved Mom from the assisted-living facility near my St. Petersburg home to a new place very near her in Sarasota.

It wasn't an easy move for Mom, bringing her yet another layer of confusion to a life filled with the unknowable. But it seemed the right thing to do, and we had to figure Mom's shrinking budget into the equation. Plus, the move made good sense in several ways. For starters, I couldn't be there for Mom every day the way I'd been there for her and Dad. Not long after Dad's death my own family moved to Western New York, where my wife had taken a faculty position at Niagara University. My son, the Down syndrome young man who'd constructed such a good life for himself, didn't want to leave Florida and start over and I couldn't blame him. More importantly, I didn't want to make life any more difficult for him than it always is, and I worried that a move might set him back.

So I became a commuter, living near the southern shore of Lake Ontario but working in Tampa, Florida. The University of South Florida, where I've been teaching for nearly twenty years, was understanding and supportive and with some contract negotiations and changes we made it work. During the semester I spend Thursdays to Mondays at home in New York with my wife and daughter, and on Monday mornings I fly south to teach and spend part of the week with my son and my teaching duties. I try to meet my family's needs as best I can, get my teaching and advising done as best as I can, keep up with my writing obligations as best I can. Mostly, I get it done.

But this meant I couldn't be there for Mom the way I'd been there for Dad and so now I've turned into one of the occasional-visitor children, like my siblings were for Dad. It's been an eye-opening experience, seeing Mom every other week for an hour or less, taking my son along with me most times. It's my sister who handles the daily routines with Mom, the financial and medical and emotional challenges that I know go with being the on-site caregiver. Me? I just show up now and again, spend a little time, give Mom a hug, and drive away.

It's a piece of cake. Mom makes few demands as her memory and her cognition slowly close in on her. She still remembers that I'm one of her children, though it's all a little vague for her and she no longer knows my name. She smiles when I come by. She seems happy enough in the reality that now is hers. She never calls, she never demands anything, and Now. The angry frustration that marked her for many months has dissipated, choked by the plaques that slowly grow on her brain. She's now on half the dosage of the anti-depressants that we started her on that noteworthy day in the doctor's office when she made it clear that she quite enjoyed beating up on Dad and planned to continue it, since it was the only way, she said, that she could make him behave. The Zyprexa and other anti-depressants calmed her down and saved Dad a lot of cuts and bruises in those final months, but the price Mom paid was a dulling of the mind, a lassitude of thought and action that was safer for both her and Dad but was sad to see. Then Dad died and so did the irritant that had created the milky pearl of anger that threatened them both. After Dad's death the phone calls from Mom—many of them angry and frenetic—ended abruptly; at first because the motivating hostility was gone, then because she was no longer capable of dialing the phone. It is incredible to me to realize that some part of me misses those calls. When she made them she was vital and passionate. Those days, those emotions, that vitality and passion, are gone.

Now, here, today, my son and I take her to a favorite bar and restaurant where the three of us sit out on the wooden deck and look out to Sarasota Bay, hoping a porpoise will swim by while we chat. On the way there she suddenly blurts out, "Eleven!"

I don't know what she means by that. "Eleven what, Mom?" I ask.

"Eleven cars," she says, and points toward the other side of the road. She's been counting the cars that go by.

"Good counting, Taffy," my Down's boy says from the backseat, reaching up to pat her on the shoulder by way of congratulation.

We drive along Macintosh Road and then get to U.S. 41, the old Tamiami Trail, as famous in its day as Route 66, a road I grew up near. On 41 we turn left and go about a mile, where we turn right on a shell road that winds its way down to the small shack of a restaurant and bar, the Spanish Point Pub, a little place with good grouper sandwiches and nice, shady umbrellas over the tables on the outdoor wooden deck. There we sip on iced tea while I tell Mom about her children, the ones she's forgotten now. I tell her how well they're doing, the daughter in California who works at Stanford, the sons in D.C. and St. Paul, both of them successful in their worlds. I remind her that her daughter Mary, a flourishing real estate agent in a place where real estate prices are rising at a dizzying pace, comes by to see her several times a week and she's surprised to find that out. I tell her about me, that I come to see her every month. I tell her that I'm a teacher and I write a little bit. She acts interested in that.

My son chimes in, telling her the news of his latest bowling scores and how much he likes having his own apartment and how he beat me yesterday in one-on-one basketball, twice, 15–14 and 15–14. I admit defeat but promise to practice harder and get him next week. He just smiles and so does Mom.

This is all news to her and she asks why no one has told her about it before, though my sister Mary, of course, tells her these sorts of things every visit. Then she smiles, takes a bite of her cheeseburger and complains that it's too big a sandwich and why don't I eat half of it? I say no thanks.

She sits back, stares at the water. She reaches out to grab her iced tea and takes a sip. She sets it down.

She smiles, she takes a bite of her cheeseburger and complains that it's too much and why don't I eat half of it? I say no thanks and start to tell her about her children and their children and their children, the generations on down the line. It's all news to her and why hasn't anyone told her about this?

My son, my Down syndrome son who's likely to face his own battle with Alzheimer's in a decade or so* unless something, a vaccine perhaps

---

*Somewhere between 40 and 100% of those with Down Syndrome will develop Alzheimer's, according to a variety of studies.

or a new miracle drug comes along, reaches over to pat her hand. "I like you, Taffy," he says. "You nice person." And she smiles and pats him back and says "I like you, too..." but then she hesitates. She can't quite remember his name. "Well, I like you, too," she says, firmly, and pats his hand.

She sips her tea. She sets it down, and I start to tell her again about her children and their children and she listens intently and wonders why no one has told her about all this.

And so we pass the time for an hour or so, my telling her again and again the things she likes to hear. Then, cheeseburger half-eaten and plenty of iced tea drunk, we get back into the car and drive her back to her assisted-living place. There, my son and I take her into her room, telling her she lives here now, popping a musical into the VCR, usually *Take Me Out to the Ball Game*, with Gene Kelly and Frank Sinatra. She likes the singing and dancing.

"I live here now?" she asks. Yes, we tell her. "And will someone come get me for dinner?" Yes, we tell her, sure, and soon.

It doesn't matter what we say, really, except that our talking keeps her happy in the moment. Her memory is perhaps fifteen seconds long, so the moment really matters. Then it's time to go. We give her a hug, my son and I, and then we walk outside into the Florida sun and heat and over to the car. And then we drive away.

Like I said; a piece of cake.

20

Cycling Out

I'M ON MY BICYCLE, a Giant hybrid, blue. It's the first week of November of 2004. I'm riding on the Pinellas Trail from Pasadena Boulevard out across the Seminole Lake bridge toward Bay Pines National Cemetery. I get off the trail on the far side of the bridge, take a left, and then a few blocks away I reach and cross Tyrone Boulevard, getting lucky and catching a green light that gets me safely across the busy intersection. Immediately I'm through the gates and into the calm, serene cemetery. I pedal for about half a mile, turn left, then left again and now I'm cycling near row after row of markers in the ground.

I get to Section C and pull the bike to a stop. I get off, set the kick-stand and walk over to my father's marker. "Delbert Wilber," it says "1919–2002."

He didn't much like to listen to me during our last year together, and so I've taken to getting my talking done when I come here to visit with him. It feels good to vent a little after I first walk around some in the quiet heat and think about what we went through, me and Dad. This particular visit, though, is very special. I've brought him some gifts.

I don't believe in ghosts. I don't believe in the afterlife. Or god. Or religion. I believe in doing the right thing when you're here. I believe in building up some good karma. Maybe I'm a Buddhist.

"Listen, you old son of a bitch," I say to him. "I've got some news. The Red Sox won the World Series."

Nothing.

"It was a pretty amazing run for them, Skip. They were down, bad, to the Yankees, but came back from that and then they just beat up on the Cardinals something awful."

Nothing, but I knew he had to have mixed feelings about that: St. Louis was his home for a long, long time and he thought of himself as an ex–Cardinal catcher just as much as he did as an ex–Sox catcher.

I sat down on the grass next to the marker.

"Listen, I know we had a rough last year together and I'm sorry about that. I'm sorry we didn't get along better. I'm sorry I couldn't always be who you wanted me to be. I'm sorry I wanted you to say 'please.'"

Nothing. I was thinking maybe I'd sense an apology from him in return, but some of the Wilber men aren't great at apologizing.

In that last year of his life I found Dad's attitude frustrating, occasionally even ludicrous. He was always testing me, and I felt like I usually failed. Did I love my father enough to serve him well no matter how he tested me? Did I love him more than I loved my children? Did I love my teaching and my writing more than his storytelling? He challenged me on all those fronts and he was often unhappy with my answers.

The combination of Dad's baseball history, his general attitude and his physical troubles led me, I admit, to hate watching the sport I grew up in and thought I'd loved so much. That isn't fair, I know. Dad's attitude was his own and from what I hear from the extended family, it was more a mark of the men in our family than it was an indictment of his ball-playing days.

Still, I connected baseball to all these troubles, and so I quit paying attention to the game almost entirely. For the first year after he died I didn't go to a single game at St. Petersburg's Tropicana Field, though it's a nice ballpark and the Rays, no matter their mediocrity, were my hometown team. I didn't watch a game, or a single pitch for that matter, on television. I paid no attention to the All-Star games and the pennant races or even the World Series.

But then, slowly, I started to drift back. Some minor-league ball, some games of catch in the front yard with my wife and daughter, a couple of Rays' games with my special son. I felt like I was healing.

And then came that remarkable run by the Red Sox, and as I watched the wins over the Yankees and the blowout of the Cardinals I began to really feel that sense for the game that I'd held for much of my life. It nagged at me as I watched: the history, the memories. Fenway in the sunshine and I was five years old. All those ballparks, all those spring trainings, all those players and their families. I couldn't blame baseball, really, for my father's tough times. I could only blame him. And blame myself.

I sat back, hands into the grass, that tough-bladed St. Augustine that's everywhere in Florida since it can stand the heat and the dry-season drought and the summer-season rains. Across the way, the road into this area of the cemetery is lined with huge, old Southern oaks: ten of them on each side, marching along militarily. I looked at the trees and the Spanish moss on their branches and thought about how nice Florida can be.

It was time. "Dad," I said, "I wanted to say thanks. For Boston. For Philadelphia. For Chicago. For Louisville and Charleston—especially for Charleston. Those years were amazing.

"And thanks for all those spring trainings. I don't suspect you knew just how much those meant to me. Indian Rocks Beach and Scottsdale, Arizona. Clearwater. St. Pete. Leaving the sleet and rain behind and heading south every spring. Damn, that was great."

I stopped for a moment, then went on: "You know, I was watching Curt Schilling pitch on that bad ankle and I was thinking of you being out there, behind the plate in Fenway, catching Sid Hudson and Ellis Kinder and, yeah, even Frank Sullivan. I remember especially that day when George Woodruff took those pictures of you and Del, Jr., and me. I was the son of a Red Sox catcher and I knew it was something special. Thank you.

"So, anyway, here's a little something for you," I said, and I placed the front page of the Boston Globe on his marker. "And here's something else." I placed the brand-new Red Sox cap on it, a special World Series champs cap. I didn't have anything to weigh these things down with, but the idea wasn't that they'd be there long. The idea was that the Red Sox had done something remarkable and Dad had been a tiny part of that Red Sox Nation once, a long time ago. And if being part of the Red Sox family and the baseball family had trapped and caged him and, in fact, trapped and caged us all, it was a trap and a cage that we had entered willingly, and some of us, most of us, were in it still, happy to be there, part of the game, part of the myth.

And then I got back on my bike, turned to wave at his grave marker and said goodbye, and pedaled off. To home, to family, to work, to real life.

Appendix:
Some Useful Resources

IF CAREGIVING COMES YOUR WAY (whether your parents were firefighters, physicians, business people, homemakers, teachers, performers or professional athletes), there are many good sources for information. I urge you to start the process of caregiving by finding out as much as you can, as soon as you can, about what caregiving is, what challenges you and your elderly parents might face, and how you might meet those challenges in a way that's best for your parents, your family, your siblings and yourself.

From a personal readings list of some fifty-four books on caregiving and its challenges, and many dozens of websites and magazine articles, here are some books, sites and articles that I found particularly useful for helping me better understand my own particular situation.

Some Excellent Books

Carr, Sasha, and Sandra Choron. *The Caregiver's Essential Handbook.* Contemporary, 2003.

> This well-organized handbook allows a new caregiver to look up information as needed, including discussions of home safety, crime protection, financial matters, health and medical treatment, communication, and taking care of yourself as caregiver. Highly recommended.

Ilardo, Joseph A., and Carole R. Rothman. *Are Your Parents Driving You Crazy?* Acton, MA: VanderWyk & Burnham, 2001.

> Ilardo and Rothman focus on methods for resolving a variety of confrontations between caregivers and elderly parents. After providing a basic method for communication, the authors pose twenty-five typical dilemmas, ranging from "My father can no longer drive safely, but he refuses to stop," to the one I found most relevant to my own situation, "My father's frequent phone calls are just too much." The plans that are offered won't always work, but knowing the dilemmas are common is helpful, and being given a tool that *may* work is helpful, as well. Highly recommended.

Lebow, Grace, and Barbara Kane, with Irwin Lebow. *Coping with Your Difficult Older Parent: A Guide for Stressed-Out Children.* New York: Quill, 2002.

> My favorite of the many books I read after my time spent as a caregiver. Lebow and Kane's guide opens with a "Difficult Parent Questionnaire" and then begins to offer techniques for handling temper tantrums, irrational demands, abusive language, manipulative and controlling behaviors, and many more. Highly, highly recommended.

Leman, Kevin. *The Birth Order Book: Why You Are the Way You Are.* 2nd ed. New York: Revell, 2004.

> Leman makes a convincing case for the impact birth order has on relationships between siblings and between children and parents. You will find yourself in these chapters, whether you are an only child, the first born of several, the middle of many, or at any other place in the family pecking order. The point is: there *is* a pecking order. The further point is that as children we work out our order in the family, but deep-seated resentments from the acceptance of that order can come out decades later under the stress of caregiving, as children vie for parental approval and the re-establishment or improvement of their place in the familial power structure. Interesting and informative.

Marcell, Jacqueline. *Elder Rage, or Take My Father ... Please!* Irvine, CA: Impressive, 2001.

> Author Marcell describes with honesty, anger, humor and sympathy her struggles with her elderly father as he declined mentally and physically. Several very useful appendices at the back of the book include "Behavior Modification Guidelines," "Long-Term Care Insurance," "Ten Warning Signs of Alzheimer's Disease," and a very direct and useful "A Physician's Guide to Treating Aggression in Dementia," by Dr. Rodman Shankle.

Marshall, John Douglas. *Reconciliation Road: A Family Odyssey.* Syracuse: Syracuse University Press, 1993; reprint Hungry Mind, 1996.

> The author travels large parts of America searching for the truth about his famous grandfather, S.L.A. (Slam) Marshall, and finds himself confronting his

own strengths and weaknesses as he struggles with the realities he finds about his grandfather. An interesting, heartfelt memoir.

Solie, David. *How to Say It to Seniors: Closing the Communication Gap with Our Elders.* Englewood Cliffs, NJ: Prentice Hall, 2004.

Solie explains the differing agendas and contexts between the elderly and their younger children or other caregivers. I found the discussions of the effect the aging process has on communication and on the understandable need for control and for a legacy particularly relevant and informative. The strategies offered in Part Three are, to my experience, on the optimistic side, but it is important that the effort be made.

Thomas, William H. *What Are Old People For? How Elders Will Save the World.* Acton, MA: VanderWyk & Burnham, 2004.

Thomas embraces the knowledge and experience that comes with aging and decries our society's focus on youthfulness. His understanding of and sympathy for the elderly is helpful not only in appreciating many of the more positive aspects of life that can only be found in older people, but also in helping caregivers understand the thought processes and emotional needs of the elderly. A chapter on "Place and No Place," which talks about the need for a place to belong and the difficulty of moving the elderly from known to unknown surroundings, is especially useful and interesting.

Tygiel, Jules. *Past Time: Baseball as History.* New York: Oxford University Press, 2000.

Tygiel's hugely interesting research into the game's realities and how they have enlarged through myth is fascinating, and his understanding of the game's role in American culture is equally absorbing. Highly recommended.

Viorst, Judith. *Imperfect Control.* New York: Simon & Schuster, 1998; paperback reprint, New York: Free Press, 1999.

Viorst continues the discussion from *Necessary Losses,* focusing in this book on power struggles between children and parents, husbands and wives, and between siblings. Learning to accepting our imperfections is enormously useful advice and the book is the stylistic equal of *Losses.* Highly recommended.

_____. *Necessary Losses.* New York: Simon & Schuster, 1986; paperback reprint, New York: Free Press, 1998.

A best-selling book and deservedly so. The book's subtitle says it all: *The Loves, Illusions, Dependencies, and Impossible Expectations That All of Us Have to Give Up in Order to Grow.* For me, particularly relevant chapters include "Good as Guilt," which helped me understand the re-emergence of old sibling rivalries; "Family Feelings," which helped me understand family myths and their power over us; "Love and Mourning," which helped me understand why I never knowingly mourned my father's death; and "I Grow Old ... I Grow Old," which helped me understand my father's "garrulous, self-centered, vapid, querulous" behaviors. You will find your own best connections to various chapters in the book. Highly Recommended.

Westbrook, Deeanne. *Ground Rules: Baseball and Myth*. Champaign: University of Illinois Press, 1996.

> Westbrook talks about baseball's role in American mythology, focusing on fathers and sons, mythic heroes, and the classis archetypes of American mythology as they are found in baseball myth. For a family steeped in baseball, an understanding of these myths and their use (and misuse) was important to me in the caregiver role and, after, with my siblings. Highly recommended for general reading on baseball.

Some Excellent Websites

1. The AARP website for caregivers is useful and informative in just about all matters pertaining to physical, emotional and financial care of the elderly. The section on caregiving is the place you should absolutely go first to begin your research. http://www.aarp.org/families/caregiving

2. The Area Agency on Aging for Pasco and Pinellas counties in Florida offers a wealth of information on caregiving: http://www.agingcarefl.org/caregiver/caregiver

3. The Family Caregiver Alliance offers information and guidance: http://caregiver.org/caregiver/jsp/home.jsp

4. The Caregiver's Home Companion site is a subscription-based site that costs $19.95 yearly for the on-line version and $29.95 yearly for the printed version. http://www.caregivershome.com/

5. Children of Aging Parents (CAPS) is a national organization out of Pennsylvania that focuses on the needs of caregiving adult children of elderly parents. http://www.caps4caregivers.org/

6. The very useful Family Support Network, out of Milwaukee, is at http://www.caregiversupportnetwork.org/. There is excellent legal and financial advice on this site.

7. Aging Parents and Elder Care, at http://www.aging-parents-and-elder-care.com/, offers beginning caregivers a very logical progression to follow from First Steps through Checklists, Daily Living and more. Extremely useful site.

8. The glossary from the Central Ohio Area Agency on Aging (COAAA) is the best concise glossary of terms that I found on the Internet. This is especially useful for new caregivers, for whom the terminology may seem,

at first, to be impenetrable. http://www.coaaa.org/index.php?go=resource&
pg=glossary

9. Writer and consultant Thomas Day offers a wealth of information
at his site, including defining in a very useful fashion the difference between
formal and informal caregiving, and the various levels of each. His discussion of The Plight of Informal Caregivers is excellent. http://www.longterm-carelink.net/eldercare/caregiving.htm

10. The Western Reserve Area Agency on Aging offers an excellent
planning guide for new caregivers: http://www.psa10a.org/Caregiving/planningforcaregiving.asp

Index

197

199